Praise For
Letters from a WWII Airman

Step into the world of a World War II radio operator as Dr. Dale Hathaway shares the biography of his father, TSgt Kenneth Hathaway. A moving collection of letters brings to life Ken's transformation from a young, inexperienced recruit to a decorated Airman in the Army Air Corps. This narrative takes us through the grueling days of training to the harrowing mission when their bomber received heavy damage from enemy fire. Interspersed throughout is a touching story of romance between Ken and the young lady he desires to marry, adding a layer of intimacy and humanity to the narrative. Perhaps most inspiring is the unwavering faith of this remarkable man, who remains steadfast in his obedience to God. This book is a must-read for anyone looking to gain a deeper understanding of the sacrifices made by the "Greatest Generation".

—**Lt Col Brian A. Wilken**, United States Air Force (Retired)

***

Sergeant Ken Hathaway was a humble, ordinary American who became a crack radio operator on a B-24 Liberator bomber during World War II. *Letters from a WWII Airman* recounts Sergeant Hathaway's story from his New England beginnings to his military draft, travels across the US for training, assignment in the European theater, and his harrowing, tragic final mission over Nazi Germany. A member of the Greatest Generation, Sergeant Hathaway's life was marked by virtuous service and Christian faith. Relying on an array of primary source documents, Dr. Dale Hathaway tells his father's story in beautifully clear, honest prose. Historians will appreciate the firsthand accounts of flight training and battle in a B-24 bomber; Christian believers will learn about how their forefathers in small churches across America cared for one another in time of national crisis, and all readers will find themselves caught up in the twists and turns of Ken and Katy's long-distance wartime romance. *Letters from a WWII Airman* is an inspirational story of humility, courage, love, family, and faith.

—**Dr. Stephen Lowe**, vice president for Academic Affairs; professor of history, *Olivet Nazarene University*

The beneficiaries of freedom have much to learn from the soldier – of commitment, of duty, of loyalty, of bravery. Their stories are told, though often reluctantly, in personal conversations, by those who served with them, and in their letters. In *Letters from a WW II Airman*, a radio operator in a B 24 Liberator bomber carries us through the rigors of training, to missions in the skies over Europe, and beyond, all while harboring a confidence nurtured by his rich faith that knits together all those admirable virtues.

—**Curt Dykstra**, whose father also served on a B-24 bomber during WW II and whose personal memories of his service are published in his book, *In the Service of My Country: I never regretted a day.*

Dr. Hathaway has written a captivating tale about a Christian young man caught up in the travails of WWII. As a history buff and fellow Christian, I found it especially interesting to read how the young man maintained his dedication to Christ while in a very worldly atmosphere. The fact that this young man was Dr. Hathaway's father and that he included information from letters and diaries personalized the story and made it very interesting reading. I highly recommend giving this book a read.

—**Lt Col Paul Dillinger**, United States Army (Retired)

My father's death in a B-24E Liberator bomber accident on May 2,1944 near Smyrna, Tennessee was a part of the WWII experience. As many men lost their lives in such accidents as did those who died in combat during the war.

Individual stories about those who served and fought for our freedoms are seldom told. Dale Hathaway's book provides an intimate and inspirational picture about his father Ken's experience in a B-24 in the European theater. This book is about faith, family and perseverance.

—**Michael LaReau**, professor emeritus, *Olivet Nazarene University*

Letters from a WWII Airman

How his faith sustained him

Dale K. Hathaway

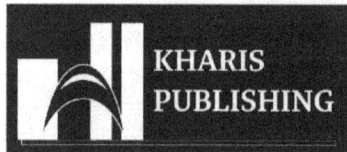

KHARIS
PUBLISHING

In memory of my dad, the best that I am I learned from him.

Acknowledgements

Few if any successful projects are done by a single individual. There is almost always a much larger group that provides feedback, encouragement, and other various types of support. I want to take a moment to thank those who have contributed to this project in one form or another.

Chaplin Dudley Hathaway, my late uncle, is the first person I want to thank. He actually summarized much of the military material from the letters he received from my dad and gave copies to all my dad's family members. It was just a terse summary of training and early war experiences, but it was the first attempt to pull parts of this story together. Maybe more importantly was when my Uncle Dud stopped by one afternoon to visit about 8 to 10 years ago, while he was passing through the area. During that visit, he presented me with a shoebox filled with letters which my dad had written to him during the war. It was a while later, during the COVID shutdown, that I took the time to read through the letters and realized that there was enough information to tell this story.

My wife Heather and my two sisters, Cher and Joy, were among the first to read the manuscript and give some feedback. Curt Dykstra, whose dad also had a book published on his B-24 experiences, read an early copy and gave significant feedback, including suggesting what became the final title of the book. I contacted my "Hathaway" cousins once the book was accepted for publication. After all, their parents are all mentioned in the book, and I wanted to make sure things were accurate and the mentions of these family members were positive. In particular, Brenda, Daphne, and Janet provided various forms of feedback and additional information related to their parents to flesh out some of the portions a little bit.

Other readers of early drafts included Michael LaReau, Lieutenant Colonel Paul Dillinger (retired), Lieutenant Colonel Brian Wilken (retired), and Dr. Stephen Lowe. A big thank you to my son-in-law, Jordan Webb who used his technical expertise to help me put together the promotion video for the book.

Finally, I would like to thank Kharis Publishing for having faith in this project and providing the resources and support to help it come to fruition: In particular, James Clement, Acquisitions & Operations Manager, Editorial team, Rufus Philips, Marketing team, Mary Hoekstra, Editorial team, and Prof. Francis E. Umesiri, Chief Editorial Officer.

I hope you enjoy this book, but even more I hope that this gives you a better understanding of the personal experiences of those who served our country so faithfully during World War II.

Dale K. Hathaway, Olivet Nazarene University, Bourbonnais, IL

Contents

Chapter 1

Introduction/Backstory

This is the true story of one Christian man who served his country during World War II. It is a story common to many from that "Greatest Generation", a story of obedience and service, training, courage, and faithfulness. In this short book you will read about the extensive training our soldiers underwent, the occasionally luxurious—but usually harsh—conditions under which they served, and the price that many paid for our freedom.

There is wartime romance in this story, as well as attempts to share what was then sensitive, censored information with family. Yet, the prevailing themes are a love of Jesus Christ and how one Christian soldier kept faithful during those dark times, including after being shot down on a bombing mission.

My father, the subject of this story, died in 2001. I regret never asking him much about his time in the war, though I heard he was reluctant to discuss those experiences.

This book is compiled from several sources. As his only son, I received the suitcase full of his WWII items, including several scrapbooks and a photo album, along with the few other items he had saved from his time in the service. A large portion of the information in this book came from letters he had written home, particularly to his youngest brother Dud, who saved every letter. A few years ago, before he too passed away, Dud shared the letters, along with some stories his big brother—my father—shared. Unless attributed to other sources, all quotes in this book are pulled from the letters my dad wrote.

If the recipient of the letter is not mentioned, then the letter is to Dud. Letters and cards to Dad from family members, friends, and acquaintances are easily identifiable. Sometimes, the chronology of the letters from Dad seems out of sequence, and this is because he often started a letter on one date, but wrote it over a few days. Also, delays in mail delivery, or in some cases letters crossing in the mail, may explain why the dates of events might not seem to match up with the letter's mention of the event.

Early Years

Milfred Kenneth Hathaway Jr. was born on August 9, 1918, in New Bedford, Massachusetts. The oldest son of Milfred Kenneth Hathaway and Isabel "Edith" Cunningham Hathaway, he went by his middle name and was known as Ken or Kenneth. Milfred Sr. was an oil burner repairman and an occasional chauffeur, and Edith was a bookkeeper, so the family was average or middle class in many ways. Over time, the family grew with Marjorie (1921) as the only daughter, Wesley Earle (1923) as the second son, and Dudley Chase (1927) as the youngest son.

Being born in 1918, my dad grew up in the 1920s and 1930s—both the Roaring Twenties and the Great Depression. The Great Depression probably had a bigger impact on my dad, given that it occurred during his late adolescent through teenage years. I know he was never very extravagant and was usually very conservative when it came to possessions and expenses, so I can only assume that his experience during this difficult period of time helped to develop that predisposition.

New Bedford is located on the Acushnet River on the southeastern coast of Massachusetts. It was officially incorporated in 1787, but English colonists had purchased the land from the Wampanoag tribe of Native Americans. Historically it is best known as a whaling town and was probably the most important whaling port at its peak, but as the whaling industry declined, New Bedford converted to a more general fishing community; today, some call it America's #1 fishing port.

The name Hathaway is also intimately tied to this community. Hathaway Road is a major thoroughfare in the greater New Bedford area. Numerous businesses have borne the name Hathaway, such as Hathaway Manor Extended Care, and Hathaway Mills, while Hathaway Home is a condo in the historic downtown. Hathaway Elementary is one of the public schools, and there is even a Hathaway Collision Center. Almost everyone has heard of Berkshire Hathaway™, which comes from the merging in 1955 of two textile companies, Berkshire based in Adams Massachusetts, and Hathaway based in New Bedford. The company is, of course, pivotal in the life of Warren Buffett.

Figure 1. Thomas R. Rodman Elementary.

Despite the prominence of the Hathaway name, my family was not directly connected to any of the Hathaway businesses, though I believe my dad did work for a Hathaway Oil Company at one point.

I do not have many records or items from his pre-war life. I know he attended C. A. Cook School (which is no longer in existence) in grades 5 through 7, and Thomas R. Rodman Elementary School for part of grade 7 and grade 8. As indicated in the class photo in Figure 1, in which he is the blonde boy in the middle of the back row, he was tall for his age and was apparently very blonde compared to the other students in his class.

I have his report cards from grades 5-8 and they indicate he was an above average student, but not a great student. His 6B grade report card indicated classroom behavior as a potential issue with him receiving P-Poor ratings every quarter for conduct, and his 8th grade report card had his prospect for promotion as C, which was only "fair" under the meaning of marks at the time.

He attended New Bedford High School and eventually graduated mid-year. During high school, he was a violin player in the orchestra his freshman year, and was a gym leader as a sophomore.

13

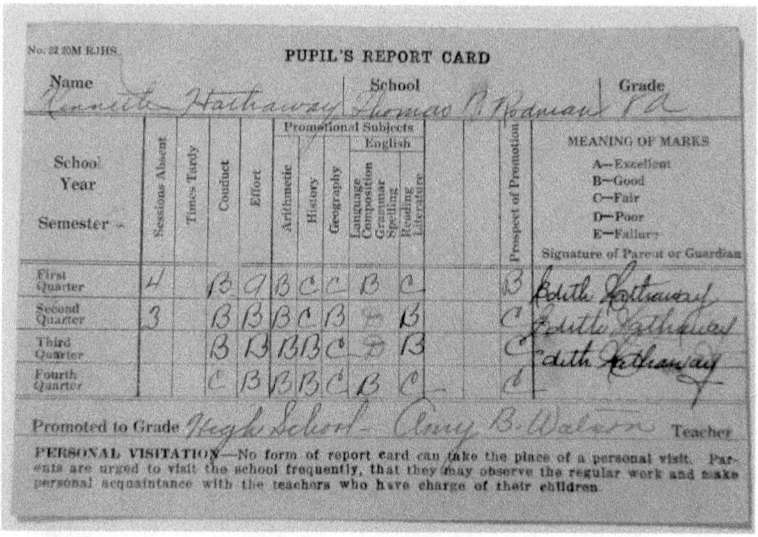

Figure 2. Rodman Elementary, 8th grade report card.

When he graduated high school, he had expressed interest in a civil service job, like working for the post office. I do not know if that ever came about, but I know that at some point he sold encyclopedias.

Chapter 2

Drafted/Initial Training

While America's entrance into the war that became known as World War II occurred because of the attack on Pearl Harbor on December 7, 1941, there was already a draft in place. On September 16, 1940, President Franklin D. Roosevelt signed the Selective Training and Service Act, which was America's first peacetime draft. With growing conflicts in Europe, many felt it was only a matter of time before America would be drawn into this new conflict. This legislation helped to expedite the process of enlarging the military to prepare for a conflict which began just a little over a year later.

It is easy to imagine tens of thousands of young men immediately entering training to help America fight for freedom after the attack on Pearl Harbor, but gearing up the military to support and train a larger force took some time. While millions of young men would eventually be trained and serve, these numbers would be spread over several years. By December 1941, Ken had already signed up for the draft and he was initially classified as "1-B", which meant "nominally available for limited military service". Here is how he described his waiting to be called up.

> Following the 'stab in the back' by the Japs at Pearl Harbor, it was only a matter of time before I was inducted into the United States Army. Being over 18 years of age I had already registered with the Selective Service. On July 21, 1941, I received my first classification which was 1-B. This classification meant that I would not be called to active service right away. I was supposed to carry this card with me at all times.

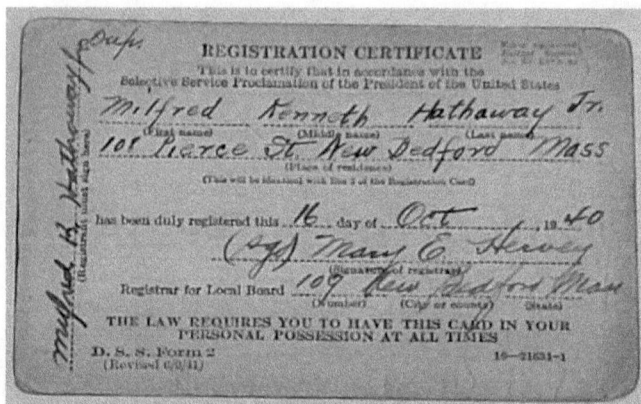

Figure 3. Ken's Original Registration Certificate.

Nearly a year later I received through the mail a notice that I had been transferred into class 1-A which meant that I would probably be called soon.

A short time later on July 16, I received my orders to report for induction on the 28th of July 1942.

The induction order (Figure 4) instructed Ken to report to the local draft board at Fire Station No. 3, Reed and Kempton Streets, New Bedford, MA. He wrote:

On Tuesday, July 28th, I reported at 7:15 A.M. at First Station #3, Reed and Kempton Streets, New Bedford Mass. From here we were taken to the depot where we took the train for Boston. I passed my physical and was inducted into the United States Army along with approximately 74 other men including Charles L. Easton, Malcom Levy, Ellsworth B. McAfee, Warren S. Bouchard, and Samuel Kaplan. My weight at this time was 128 lbs. Following our induction we were given twelve days furlough.

The others which Ken listed by name were individuals that he and his family knew. In the early weeks of training, he often included items like his weight. Ken was close to six feet tall, but he was very slim with a weight of only 128 lbs.

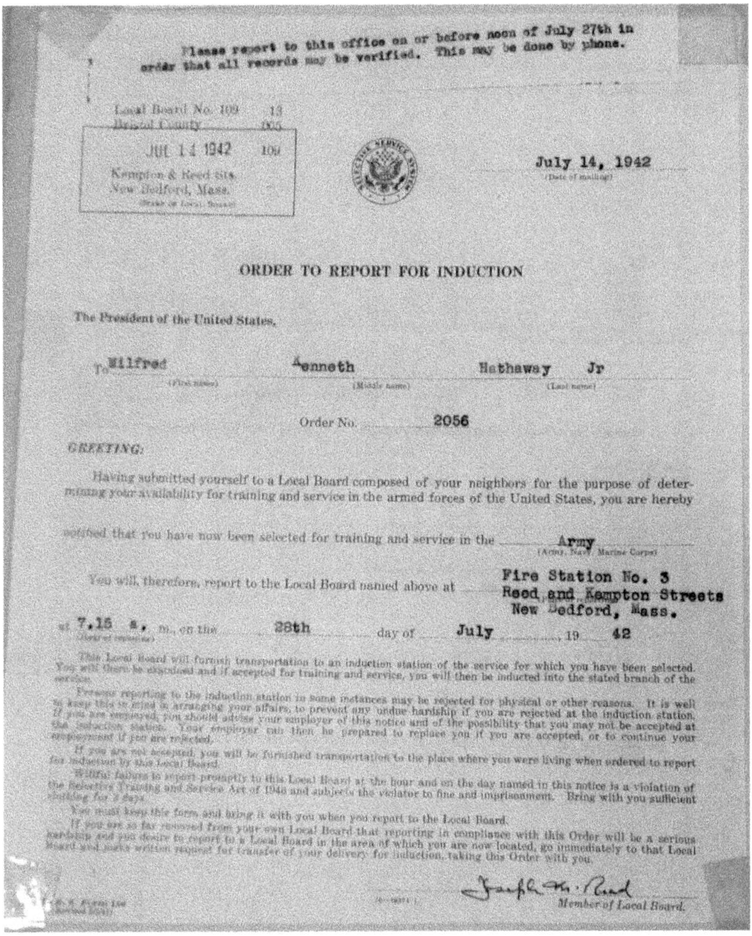
Please report to this office on or before noon of July 27th in order that all records may be verified. This may be done by phone.

Local Board No. 109
Bristol County
JUL 14 1942
Kempton & Reed Sts.
New Bedford, Mass.

July 14, 1942

ORDER TO REPORT FOR INDUCTION

The President of the United States,

To Wilfred Kenneth Hathaway Jr

Order No. 2056

GREETING:

Having submitted yourself to a Local Board composed of your neighbors for the purpose of determining your availability for training and service in the armed forces of the United States, you are hereby notified that you have now been selected for training and service in the Army

You will, therefore, report to the Local Board named above at Fire Station No. 3 Reed and Kempton Streets New Bedford, Mass.

at 7.15 a. m., on the 28th day of July, 1942

This Local Board will furnish transportation to an induction station of the service for which you have been selected. You will there be examined and if accepted for training and service, you will then be inducted into the stated branch of the service.

Persons reporting to the induction station in some instances may be rejected for physical or other reasons. It is well to keep this in mind in arranging your affairs, to prevent any undue hardship if you are rejected at the induction station. If you are employed, you should advise your employer of this notice and of the possibility that you may not be accepted at the induction station. Your employer can then be prepared to replace you if you are accepted, or to continue your employment if you are rejected.

If you are not accepted, you will be furnished transportation to the place where you were living when ordered to report for induction by this Local Board.

Willful failure to report promptly to this Local Board at the hour and on the day named in this notice is a violation of the Selective Training and Service Act of 1940 and subjects the violator to fine and imprisonment. Bring with you sufficient clothing for 3 days.

You must keep this form and bring it with you when you report to the Local Board.

If you are so far removed from your own Local Board that reporting in compliance with this Order will be a serious hardship and you desire to report to a Local Board in the area of which you are now located, go immediately to that Local Board and make written request for transfer of your delivery for induction, taking this Order with you.

Joseph M. Reed
Member of Local Board.

Figure 4. Induction order.

On Monday morning, August 10, 1942, one day after his 24th birthday, he reported once again to Fire Station #3 in New Bedford. A bus took the recruits to the train station where he was met by Ma and Dad, Marge, Dud, Aunt Annie, Hetty and John Bouchard, Mr. Lee, Irene Allen, Joe Baker, Dot Grew, Mr. Gatie, and Muriel. Muriel was a female friend from church. They were not really seriously dating, but it was clear from later communication that Muriel had strong feelings for Ken, though his feelings for her were not of the same magnitude. They stood around and talked for a while but soon the train pulled up and he had to say goodbye to all the folks.

August 13, 1942:

As I climbed into the train, I waved to everyone and was soon on my way to the reception center at Fort Devens by way of Boston. We reached

Fort Devens at 1 p.m. and then things really started to happen. Following dinner we had our I.Q. test. At 11 p.m. I retired for the first time as an active soldier in Uncle Sam's Army.

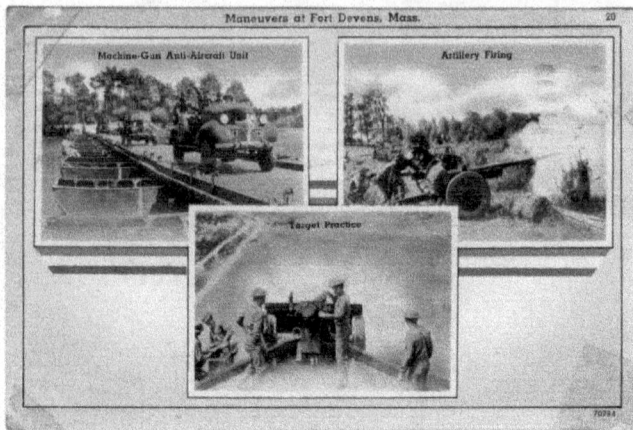

Figure 5. A post card from Fort Devens.

August 11, 1942:

The next day we had an intelligence test (a different test than the I.Q. test from the previous day) and I was chosen for the Air Corps which meant that I rated pretty high in my test as only the highest were chosen for the Air Corps. We were then issued our G.I. clothes, both summer and winter. Having no more need for our civilian clothes we packed them and sent them home. By the time I retired I had had two inoculations, I had two blisters on my feet and instep was bleeding from a floor burn.

August 12, 1942:

Where I was inoculated my arm felt like a heavy weight and hurt all day. Most of the fellow's arms were pretty sore. Couldn't touch them.

Fort Devens, located about 60 miles northwest of Boston, was used as an initial induction site, where soldiers go through some preliminary items like the IQ test and inoculations before they quickly relocated elsewhere for their initial training. As is often the case in the military, the soldiers themselves were not given any information as to their next location.

August 15, 1942:

On August 12, we got our barracks bag ready to leave. We had to walk to the station one and one half miles away with our 65 lb. bag on our backs. My arm was still hurting from the inoculations the day before. We departed from Fort Devens at 10 a.m. with no knowledge of our destination. We reached our destination, Atlantic City, New Jersey, at 7:30 p.m. In a pouring rain we walked 1 ½ miles to the hotel where we stayed for one week.

Atlantic City, New Jersey

Ken could not give the name of the hotel in which they stayed but he did describe the hotel as "one of the best".

In a postcard to his brother Wes, he said, "…must address all my mail to Milfred instead of Kenneth" to ensure that he would receive the mail. One of the downsides of not going by his given first name is that everyone had been writing to him as Ken or Kenneth, but to the military he was Milfred.

Throughout the war Ken wrote extensively, but especially over these early days when he did not yet know many others. Also, because of weather and the status of their training, he had a fair amount of spare time. In a letter from August 13, 1942, he commented that it was still raining and they were confined to the hotel for at least 8 days when not training. But despite the weather they still had to do some training and were walking 10 miles a day and they had to learn the 12 rules of conduct word for word.

August 13, 1942:

Am in the Air Corps and will be in the Air Corps for the remainder of the war. This does not mean necessarily we will fly but will be in the ground crew or connected in some way with the Air Corps. The Air Force is the best branch of the service and only those with the highest I.Q. get in.

We will be here for at least two weeks for our basic training. After that we will be assigned to what we are to do and will probably be shipped out again.

My blisters were pretty bad Wednesday and was going out on Sick Call but hated to miss anything. They are better today. Have a handkerchief wrapped around them.

Ken stating that while he was in the Air Corps that did not mean that he would fly was correct. The Army Air Force regulations required four technical specialists for every man who flew. When other ground personnel were accounted for there were approximately sixteen individuals who served in a noncombat roles for every one crewman who saw combat.

Figure 6. K.P. Duty post card.

Lots of soldiers training hard meant the need for plenty of food, so Ken got the inevitable KP (kitchen patrol) duty, just like most other soldiers did at one point or another.

August 16, 1942:

On August 16, at 6:00 p.m. I went on K.P. for my first time with four others and we shucked 2,600 ears of corn and cut out the bad places and also cut 9,000 potatoes and picked over 5 crates of lettuce and 3 bushels of tomatoes. We then toasted 3 bushel buckets of bread over the stove and boy was it hot!

As we came off duty the next day at 5 a.m. having been without sleep for 25 ½ hours, we were told that we had to take four more examinations before we could get any sleep. By the time we reached the place of the examinations (it was a mile away) we had been 27 hours without sleep.

The first test was a mechanical exam which lasted 20 minutes. The second was also a mechanical exam which lasted 30 minutes. Third was a thirty-minute exam on Morse Code. This exam was in two parts each having seventy eight questions. Finally came the main exam of all. Those who passed this test high enough got a chance to go to technical school to qualify for Photographer, Aerial Gunner, Machine Gunner, mechanic, and others. This would give them a rating of T/Sgt at $25 a week. This was a mathematical examination which had only twenty questions but it took two hours. I got seventeen right and guessed at the other three, two of which I was pretty sure. When I retired at 6 p.m. I had gone 36 ½ hours without sleep and had lost 6 lbs.

Figure 7. Post card of the President's Hotel.

Over the next few days they did calisthenics, drilled, and had lectures on topics like military courtesy and gas masks, along with other basic training, both physical and mental. On Wednesday, August 19, they moved to a new location further down the boardwalk, the 12-story President Hotel, though Ken thought it was not as nice as the previous hotel.

With the move to the new hotel they were no longer restricted to the hotel when not training. Evidently the hotel had some say in the restrictions placed upon the recruits who stayed there. Being off restrictions, Ken was now able to get out.

August 22, 1942:

Last night they had a free concert for the soldiers, about 2500 went. We had Mal Hallett and his orchestra play for an hour. A little jazzy but mostly good war songs. I met Paul K. as it let out and (he) told me he was staying at another hotel. We are off restrictions and can go out anywhere not out of the city until 10:00 P.M. Paul K. is still on restriction. It's more or less up to the hotel. We have made plans to meet in front of the Marlborough-Blenheim at 8:00 A.M. Sunday and go to church. Probably the Salvation Army as we have no church near here.

Some of their training days were long and hard, but that is what it takes to get a soldier ready for combat.

August 22, 1942:

Well I am back again it is 6:30 P.M. and what a day we put in. At 8:30 A.M. after waiting around, they seem to be all mixed up here, we had a different instructor each day, we filed out to the drill field a mile walk. For 2 ½ hrs. we drilled and exercised and ran. We were certainly tired when we pulled into the hotel for dinner (lunch). Had a very good dinner, we had only an hour for dinner and marched over to another drill field. For over 3 hours in the blazing sun, about 90 out, we drilled with only two ten minute rest periods. It was all dirt and very dusty, we were filthy with dirt and dog tired. On our feet marching and drilling for more than 3 hours. We had a tough instructor but a good one and he kept us going. We are all eager to learn though. We had supper at 5:00 P.M. I took a bath, shaved and shined my shoes and am now writing.

The army life isn't so bad and you certainly get plenty of walking. Am catching up on sleep and have all day tomorrow off as far as I know unless I get K.P. again. I hope not; once is enough for a while.

The Herald of Holiness was a publication of the Church of the Nazarene, and as a church member, Ken subscribed to the periodical even while in the military. It is referenced several times in this book, and is one of several things which show his commitment to church.

August 22, 1942:

Have received no Herald as yet but am waiting to receive as next Sunday may get leave for a day and be able to go out of the city to a Nazarene Church.

Even though he was staying and training in New Jersey, his Boston Red Sox allegiance rang true.

August 22, 1942:

Too bad the Red Sox couldn't have taken the Yankees in that doubleheader, losing the second game 2-1. Can't keep up with baseball too much as we don't get a paper all the time. It costs too much to get one every day.

As this next incident seems to indicate, there were inevitable training accidents, especially for those in the air corps.

August 22, 1942:

This afternoon while we were drilling we heard an explosion and pile of black smoke overhead. It occurred at the airport which is only ½ mile away. No authentic report yet as to what caused it. Might have been a plane crash. We have bombers, pursuit planes, seaplanes and private planes flying overhead constantly. 14 bombers at one time occasionally.

While in Atlantic City, NJ, Ken actually met a family member! His younger sister Marjorie (or Marge) had been attending a camp in Pennsylvania with a friend, but on the way back to New Bedford, MA, they had stopped off in Atlantic City to see if Marge could find her big brother.

August 22, 1942:

Last night who do you suppose I saw but Marjorie and Florence. Out of around 40,000 soldiers, I don't know how many are here but it seems like that many, she found me. I was out on the boardwalk about 9:30 P.M.

They wanted me to meet them this morning. We were up at 6:00 A.M. were told we had 2 1/2 hours detail work, cleaning first floor and washing it. I asked Corporal Leslie if I could be excused and he let me see them off. Hope they didn't get tired standing up. I got back to the hotel at 8:30 A.M. At 9:00 A.M. was called out on another detail. Had to be a runner for the Sergeant downstairs. Anything or anybody he wanted I went and got him. Had to take a three-mile hike to deliver some papers to another squadron.

Even this early in their training, they might receive a variety of miscellaneous assignments. A runner was just mentioned and certainly the earlier KP assignment, but another possible duty which Ken received several times in the service was being assigned as CQ.

August 22, 1942:

One night that I especially remember was the night I spent as C.Q. (charge of quarters). I sat in one corner of the hotel all night and made sure that everything was all right. The wind blew about sixty miles an hour. The streets were flooded and it was lightning and pouring. The storm continued to get worse as the night wore on. I was frozen even though I had on my trench coat and could hardly keep awake.

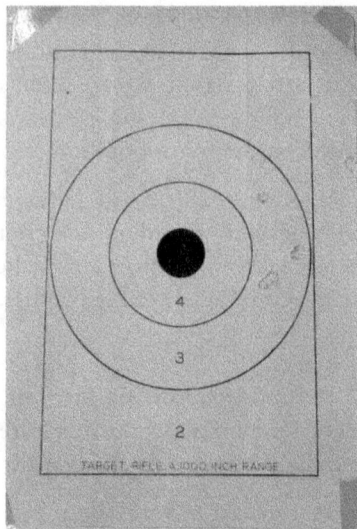

Figure 8. The first target Ken shot in the Army.

Everyone in the military had to learn how to fire a rifle, even if they would end up in a position like being part of the air corps ground crew, which was not likely to see combat. The following was Ken's first experience in the army firing a gun, but I think he miscounted, because the target appears to show that 5 shots actually made a score; there are two places where it appears that two shots were almost right on top of each other.

August 25, 1942:

Well we filed out to the yard and were told we were going to have rifle practice. We left here at 9:00 A.M. and marched 4 1/2 miles to the other drill field I mentioned in my previous letter. From there we walked about ½ mile further and Army trucks picked us up and carried us three more miles to the rifle range. We carried our canteen on our belt filled with water and they gave us three sandwiches and an orange in a bag as we weren't coming back for dinner. The sandwiches were two ham and one jelly.

We arrived at the rifle range and after about ½ hour took our place on the firing line with an instructor by our side. We each had 15 shots and only 4 of mine made a score, 2 hit outside of the target. I am enclosing the target. Save it as a souvenir. The first shot was the worse. We had 5 lying face down, five sitting, and five standing. I fired the first one and back came the rifle against my shoulder. What a kick. After the first three my shoulder didn't hurt any more but it will be sore tomorrow morning. As you fire the rifle it kicks so hard the gun goes almost out of your hand

and upward. They have every precaution against an accident. It was fun. We might go out again if we stay long enough.

We marched 4 ½ miles back after the trucks had taken us back to the drill field. We arrived back to the hotel at 3:00 P.M. and drilled 1 ½ hrs. on the beach. We are pretty tired but getting used to it fast.

We were informed tonight we must stand inspection by the captain tomorrow morning and Tuesday a final training inspection by the colonel. Everything must be perfect in regards to uniform and appearance. We were informed we must wear our winter uniforms for the inspection. Sept 15th everyone must wear the winter uniforms at all times while off duty on our part.

While I think of it I tried to iron my pants tonight, the winter ones. I have two pair and scorched them a little. Is there any possible way to removing the scorched part? Let me know if there is.

It is hard not to laugh at reading the last part about scorched pants. There was no later correspondence about the answer he received, but his family assumed he got it straightened out prior to the final training inspection. How many new soldiers have had something similar happen early in their military service?

The intense drilling and training took their toll on the soldiers, especially since the training happened no matter what the weather was like. War happens under all atmospheric conditions, so soldiers train during all types of weather. Ken got physically sick because of the weather/training conditions.

August 27, 1942:

I took sick this morning on the drill field. I felt like throwing up and had a headache, then I had a case of the chills. When I got back to the hotel I went in for dinner but only ate the dessert, cherry pie. It was good. I then reported for sick call and went over to the hospital. My temperature was over 100. I was ordered back to my room for the rest of the day. ... At 4:30 decided to go down and try to eat some supper. They had hamburger balls, potato, string beans and milk and cake. It looked so good. I ate a regular supper. It is now a little after five and I feel lots better, will probably go to bed early tonight and will feel all right in the morning. Almost everyone has a cold. No matter how cold it is out at drill field we have to take off our shirt and exercise in our undershirt, we also have to lie down. No wonder we catch cold.

The training kept the soldiers busy, too busy to get very homesick, but that did not mean they never thought about the life they used to have.

Figure 9. Post card on how soldier's feet feel after a long hike.

August 27, 1942:

We don't have much time to think of home but once in a while think about it and wish I could get home for a day or so.

Soldiers were subjected to strenuous physical training they needed to get them in shape. These recruits came from many different walks of life, but it was also to ensure they were ready to face the hardships that come with war. The impact of such constant physical exertion on a body that is not ready for it can lead to a breakdown. Here Ken shared the impact of the training on his body after being in the service for just over two weeks.

August 28, 1942:

Woke up and couldn't straighten right leg out. Couldn't walk on right foot but limped to the hall to answer roll call. Went back to bed. At 8:00 a.m. was woken up by the Sick Call corporal who wanted to know why I didn't answer sick call. I told him I couldn't walk so he helped me down stairs and called an ambulance which took me to the hospital. The doctor looked at my leg and sent me to bed. He said it was slightly infected and told me to bathe it with Epsom Salts for 15 minutes every four hours.

August 29, 1942:

Woke up with a badly swollen right leg, still in hospital.

August 30, 1942:

Still in hospital – Foot still badly swollen but no pain.

September 1, 1942:

Still in hospital – supposed to be discharged today but still can't walk perfect – put shoes on for the first time since Friday.

The training was physically challenging, but it was mentally challenging as well.

August 27, 1942:

While I was at the hospital they brought in a fellow unconscious. He became dizzy and fell and cut his head. He was unconscious over a half hour. They called an ambulance and took him out still unconscious. Another Southern fellow is being confirmed to the psycho ward. He isn't a bad case just minor. It's a case of nerves.

Ken's time in the hospital because of his leg and foot meant he was not able to ship out at the same time as the other recruits who had arrived with him.

September 4, 1942, Friday:

Out of hospital but feet not right yet – Most of the gang shipped out. Drilled.

Soldiers were worked hard, but there was entertainment to balance things out. Ken wrote:

On September 5 I saw Glenn Miller and his band. The next day (9/6) I went to Egg Harbor to church. (9/7) On Labor Day we walked two miles to the hospital and had a shot in each arm. Five fellows fainted including the one in front of me. I spent September 9 on K.P. once more (wakened at 3 a.m., with K.P. from 4 a.m. until 6:30 p.m.). This time I worked 14 ½ hours and washed 3,000 cups and dishes and 1,000 cereal bowls. We drill for the first time with rifles (10 lbs.) on Thursday (9/10) (weight 130).

This book is constructed from letters, mostly letters Ken wrote home, but that is only one side of the communication. Ken's spirit was constantly uplifted by the communications he received from friends and family back home. Mrs. Matilda Costa sent the first card he received in the service, and she ended up being one of the most faithful card and letter writers, despite her comment of not being good at letter writing. She was a lady from the church back home, and as such, much of her communication had a spiritual connection, as did so many of the other cards and letters he received.

August 1942, card from Mrs. Costa:

I am no good at letter writing so I am sending this card. I will be praying for you. Write when you have time. God bless you and keep you.

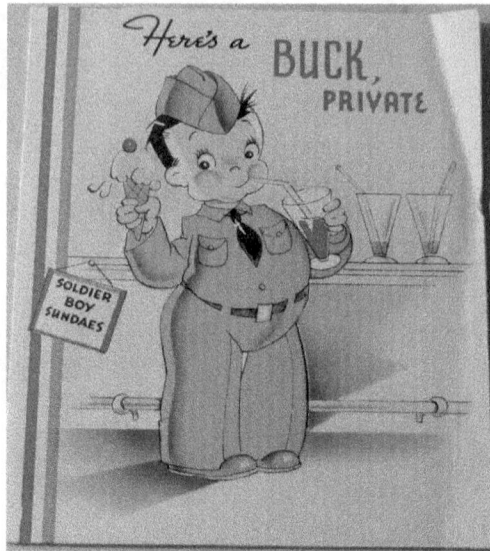

Figure 10. An early card Ken received.

Sept 1942, card from Mrs. Costa:

Wish you lots of luck in your new life (for it is something new to you) and pray for you that your stay will be a short one and soon this awful war will be over. God bless you and keep you. Hope we may see you soon.

Sept 1942 card from Curt:

We are all remembering you in our prayers Ken and expect the Lord to be with you and give you grace.

September 6, 1942, letter from Aunt Luna:

Aunt Elsie intends to write you as soon as possible, she received your good letter, and we were both pleased to hear from you, but regretted to learn of your physical handicap, however it is nothing strange as you have not been accustomed to do such strenuous things in the past.

Surely these are very trying days that we are living in, and one never knows what a day will bring forth. But God is still on His throne and answers the cry of His children. I want to be always ready and waiting for whatever I may be called upon to go through. For one thing I know, it pays to be true.

The initial stage of training was winding down, though they still did not know where they might be sent for the next portion of their training.

September 12, 1942:

Inspection by the Captain in the morning – in the afternoon drilled in preparation for our final inspection by the Colonel Tuesday.

On Sunday, September 13, detail work in morning, I went to Saint Paul's Methodist Church, Ohio and Pacific Avenues, Atlantic City. Rev. W. W. Payne was the minister.

September 14, 1942:

Drilled hard all day – Final inspection postponed until Wednesday.

September 15, 1942:

Drilled hard in the morning – dress parade in the afternoon – 7 p.m. someone came in and told me I was on the shipping list so I reported to the shipping clerk and he told me to stay in my room and be ready to leave on a minutes notice.

Chapter 3

Training/Illinois

After the initial training in Atlantic City, Ken shipped out on September 16, 1942 to the next stage of his training. As usual, the soldiers themselves did not know where they were headed.

September 16, 1942, Departed Atlantic City:

I shipped out of Atlantic City on Wednesday, September 16, at 1:30 p.m. We went in trucks to a building where we were assigned to our car. We left at 5:30 p.m. our destination again unknown. While traveling to our next station we went through Pittsburgh, Columbus, across Indiana and across Illinois arriving at Scott Field at 11 p.m. September 17.

While passing through Indiana he sent three postcards which said: "Ma Look at the Postmark. Don't know where we are going. Kenneth". The first was postmarked Columbus Indiana, the second was postmarked

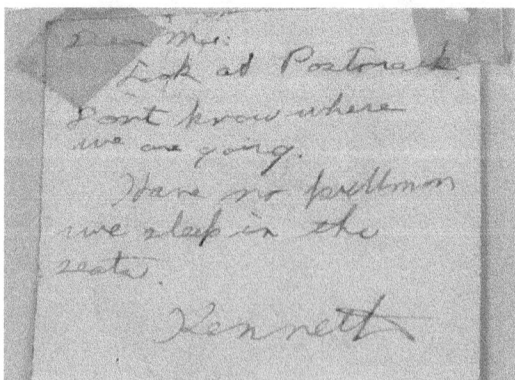

Figure 11. The third post card he sent while traveling through Indiana. postcard to Ma while enroute from NJ.

New Albany, Indiana and said: "Ma: Look at the postmark. Am still traveling. Weather good. Got three hours sleep last night sitting up. Will write a letter

30

as soon as I get to my destination. Kenneth". The third, shown in Figure 11, was postmarked Franklin, Indiana, and said: "Dear Ma: Look at the Postmark Don't know where we are going. Have no Pullman we sleep in the seats. Kenneth".

Upon arrival to Scott Field (now the US Airbase near Belleville, IL) the recruits were assigned to tents for the first few days. Given the time of year, the temperatures were probably not too bad, but other weather-related issues were more challenging, including waking up one morning with a 6 by 8 inch puddle on his blanket. It appeared that often the newest soldiers were the ones assigned duties like KP, since Ken arrived on September 17, but on September 19 had KP from 3:00 a.m. until 8 p.m.

On September 21, 1942, Ken was assigned to the 93rd Technical School Squadron and a few days later was told that he would be going to radio operator and mechanic school.

In a new place surrounded by soldiers that he may not have known previously, some of the conversations between soldiers became quite interesting. Ken was a member of the Nazarene denomination, a fairly conservative denomination which emerged in North America from the 19th-century Wesleyan-Holiness movement within Methodism. It is the largest denomination in the world aligned with the Wesleyan-Holiness movement and has its headquarters just outside Kansas City, KS. Ken was not afraid to have conversations with those of other beliefs and denominations.

September 23, 1942:

We got on a discussion of religion in our tent last night, a Jew, a congregationalist and myself. They said they didn't know there was any body that didn't believe in drinking, smoking, movies, dancing, etc. We discussed it quite a bit and the congregational fellow saw my point of view in a number of ways. He is going to one of our churches with me.

At that time, numerous activities like drinking, smoking, and movies were prohibited within the Nazarene denomination, not necessarily because they are wrong or evil, but in some cases because of the possibility of leading others astray. Movies at that time were shown in buildings that at other times might have had far more questionable activities. The idea was not that movies were bad; instead, this prohibition had more to do with not wanting to indirectly support other more questionable activities. In other situations, like with alcohol, the idea follows this passage:

Be careful, however, that the exercise of your rights does not become a stumbling block to the weak. For if someone with a weak conscience sees you, with all your knowledge, eating in an idol's temple, won't that person be emboldened to eat what is sacrificed to idols? So this weak brother or

31

sister, for whom Christ died, is destroyed by your knowledge. When you sin against them in this way and wound their weak conscience, you sin against Christ. Therefore, if what I eat causes my brother or sister to fall into sin, I will never eat meat again, so that I will not cause them to fall (1 Corinthians 8:9-13, New International Version)

Nowadays within the Nazarene denomination, the movie restriction is gone, and the dangers of smoking are well documented, but the prohibition of alcohol is still in place in the spirit of that 1 Corinthians passage.

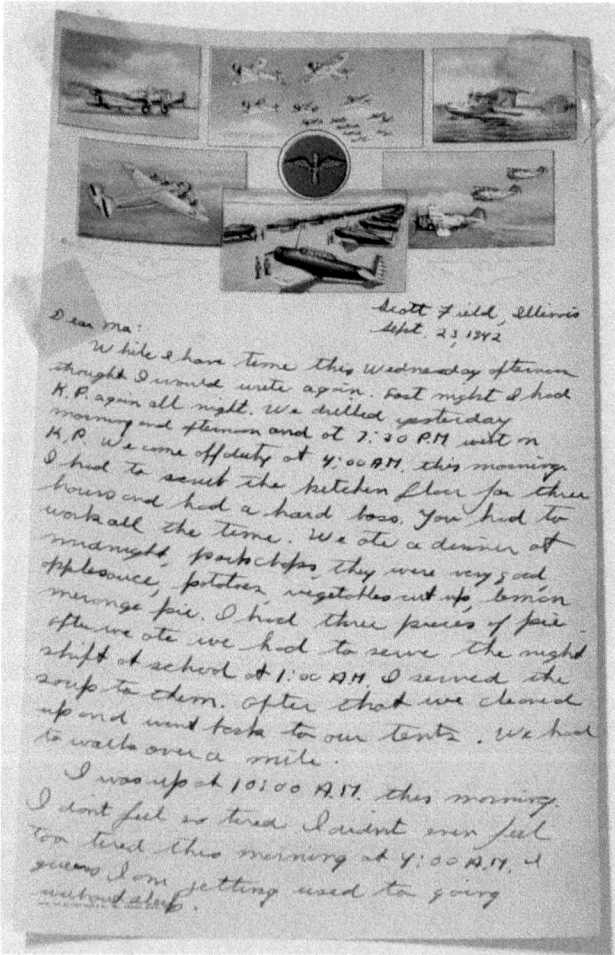

Figure 12. The first page of Ken's September 23, 1942 letter on military letterhead.

The next few weeks seemed to be pretty uneventful and routine, with days filled with drilling, duties, and occasional entertainments. The drilling usually involved a lot of hiking and calisthenics, but also included things like running obstacle courses and having a tug of war. Ken also mentioned playing volleyball several times, probably as more of a relaxation activity than part of the drilling.

Over the next few weeks Ken was assigned to various duties including KP, standing guard duty, and mopping up around the barracks. But they also had time for other more pleasant activities. On Sunday September 27, Ken was given the day off and was able to attend a protestant church service, which I assume was on the base. On Wednesday September 30, he was able to go to a USO show in the evening.

Figure 13. A card from Muriel with a long letter.

Early in Ken's time in the service, Muriel, the girl he knew from his church back home, sent him a number of cards and items, all indicating her desire for a deeper relationship, including the card and letter in Figure 13 which said: "To My Boy Friend in the Service" and the note in Figure 14 below.

Ken did not view Muriel as a girlfriend, but based on the cards and letters she sent to him, I think it is safe to say that she had a strong desire for the relationship to be more than just friendship. But as friends he did write her and, as indicated below, tried to ensure that she received some pictures of him in the military.

October 11, 1942:

You can have more made and give Muriel a set as she wants some. We can't get reprints here on the post, some army rule, and so will have to wait until I get out.

The training at this point was still fairly basic.

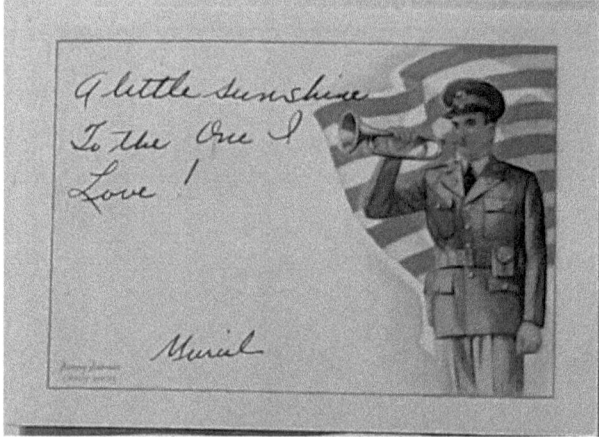

Figure 14. A short note from Muriel.

October 4, 1942:

Had a lecture at 7:45 – Also movies of a bombing raid on Germany showing what our duties will be when we go across in about 6 to 8 months."

October 5, 1942:

Exercises in the morning - Started school – From 3 p.m. until 7:15 p.m. we study theory or mechanics in radio with laboratory work every other day or so. We have one hour for supper from 5:15 to 6:25 at 7:15 we move to our code school and there learn the code and by the use of earphones practice receiving and sending code. We get out of school at 10:45 p.m.

Ken excelled at receiving and sending code; this would play a role in some of his later assignments.

October 7, 1942:

In the morning had exercises and played volleyball – went to school in the afternoon and the instructor told me that I am the best in the class so far and that I would soon be in the next class.

Ken always tried to attend church services and even got his picture taken by the chapel on the base (Figure 15). He also tried to hang out with those with similar interests.

October 11, 1942:

I went to church this morning here at the post. Had a good service and am going to try and go tonight again. They have a Christian Endeavor program at night for an hour.

Figure 15. Ken getting his picture taken in front of the chapel at the base.

About the picture ... The big fellow on the left is the one I told you about walking with one Sunday. He likes to associate with somebody who doesn't drink.

There were plenty of inoculations. Since soldiers would be traveling to different parts of the world, various shots were needed to cover things that we thankfully did not have to experience back in the states.

October 11, 1942:

I have to have two more shots. These are only good for one year so if I am still in at the end of a year will have to take them all over. Also if I go across I get one for yellow fever. They jab this one in your rear end and practically everybody is sick from it for a couple of days. I don't expect to have KP so much now that I am in school. Maybe once every four or five weeks.

Figure 16. Ken at Scott Field. He claimed the wind was blowing fiercely and that is why his pants look so baggy.

While there are some that might question a good Christian man going to USO shows, they were fairly clean and wholesome, though some movies and films might now portray them as a little more questionable. This comment from Ken seemed appropriate and fitting.

October 11, 1942:

Most of the USO shows are pretty good. The only reason I went is to have some diversion seeing as I couldn't get out of here. As a rule these are pretty good.

Sometimes it was hard to communicate the details of things through the mail, and of course he had to always be aware of the censors, who cut out material which they felt was inappropriate, but in this next passage Ken tries to give a bit more information on the training and his possible future assignments. He had no say in what he would do, but he was interested in a preferred, or safer, position.

October 11, 1942:

I will explain the situation on the Aerial Gunnery School if I can. It is easier to tell them than to write about it. If I don't go to Aerial Gunnery School or RL on graduation from here, I may either fly or do ground work. I made a mistake the other day, the majority stay on the ground. If by chance I do fly I will not have had the machine gun experience that Aerial Gunnery School gives you, so your chances are less. If I thought I was going to fly would go to Aerial School but there is no way of telling so I am sort of on the fence. However I don't think I will go to Aerial Gunnery School but will graduate and take a chance on being put on the Ferry Command. That is another thing that is just luck, you can't ask for it if you get it O.K. if you don't you don't. In the Ferry Command you take bombers across to foreign countries, that is the job I would like. A little action but not so much danger as an aerial gunner in a plane. A little less dangerous than a radio operator though I believe. You get your regular pay plus 50% for flying time and $6.00 a day additional as you don't live on any post. So you make about $70.00 a week.

Ken continued to do well in the training and excelled at typing.

October 11, 1942:

I might say that out of my class of 50 I was the first to graduate from typing four words a minute to typing 8 words a minute. You have to type 16 to pass. I went to 8 words a minute in three days and expect to go to 10 in a couple of days. In my theory class or mechanical had two tests. I got a 95% and 84%. In my laboratory experiments don't know what I got yet but I'm not so good in that.

October 12, 1942:

In code class graduated once again from 8 words a minute to 10 words a minute. Still the best radio operator in the class – only one in a class of 50 to be on 10 words a minute.

October 14, 1942:

Went to school in the afternoon and passed 10 words a minute and am now on 12 words a minute.

The army was still the army and a stickler for those who don't do things up to their standards. Having to clean the entire barracks because of dust on one window sill probably helped Ken not to make that mistake again.

October 17, 1942:

Had to clean entire barracks because I didn't wipe the dust off the window sill yesterday – changed to winter uniforms.

Ken always wrote extensively about his Sunday church experiences. He was a devoted Christian, as was his family, and this was a topic he could share without fear of censorship and it was a topic of interest to his family.

Figure 17. A card Ken received that was both Christian and military.

October 18, 1942:

On Sunday, October 18, I left camp at 7:30 a.m. for St. Louis. I took the bus to Belleville (about 9 miles away) and then hitchhiked with another fellow into St. Louis. I arrived at the church at 9:40 a.m. by trolley ten minutes late for Sunday school. There were about twenty-five young people in the class I was in. There were 502 out to Sunday School and the offering was twelve dollars. At church there were about 350. After Church Billy MacKay, who was also at church (he was also stationed at Scott Field) introduced me to a couple around forty years of age with whom he usually eats on Sunday. Their name was Wakefield. They drove us in their 1941 Chevrolet to a sister of the wife and we had dinner there. After dinner we went for a 2 hour ride down to a lake and watched the sailboats and speedboats for a while. Missed the N.Y.P.S. service which starts at 6:45. At night Rev. Roach the pastor preached another fine service at 7:45. There were about 400 out. Rev. Roach has been there 16 years.

This is the first mention of the Wakefields. Over the next few months he would spend a good portion of his time off in the St. Louis area and would often mention the Wakefield's as where he spent the day or where he had a meal. They were a very hospitable family to Ken while he was stationed at Scott Field.

Ken's parents evidently were able to travel out to see him. There were no details other than they were there from October 24 to November 7. It is a bit surprising, as a trip from Massachusetts to Illinois would not have been easy or inexpensive for his family, and of his siblings, Ken's youngest brother still lived at home. Since his parents were there and he was spending his time with them, he did not write many letters during this time. He mentioned his parents' visit in his next letter to his brother Dud.

October 11, 1942:

Thought I would write a short letter tonight. It seems funny staying in tonight instead of being out with Ma and Dad.

One thing that is so obvious in looking through Ken's old letters is his commitment to his faith. In some scrapbooks there are more church and revival programs than there are military related items. He certainly was a committed Christian with a strong love of the Lord. During the week of November 8, the St. Louis church was holding revival services with Nettie Miller (1897-1950, evangelist, Church of the Nazarene), which meant services every evening, and Ken tried to attend as many as possible.

November 8, 1942:

Sunday night went to church. They had 583 out to S.S. and are trying for 675 this Sunday. I believe they will make it. Sunday night had a great service. The altar was lined and they had a capacity crowd. They turned some away. They had around 700 out.

November 10, 1942:

The following Tuesday when I went to church I was invited to stay overnight with a man who was at church. His home was a two room trailer in a trailer park. I spent quite a few nights there.

November 11, 1942:

After a good night's sleep in Clarence's trailer, I spent the day at the Wakefields' and then went to church again at night and had another wonderful service. Went to church Friday night also. On Sunday there were around a thousand at church with only standing room. They had 747 out to Sunday School.

November 13, 1942:

Got a pass and went into church and had a wonderful service.

One of the most famous names associated with the USO during World War II was Bob Hope. Ken did get to see him at least once.

November 16, 1942:

On Monday night, November 16, I saw Bob Hope in one of the hangers. There were 7,000 there.

Ken's training work continued to go well.

November 23, 1942:

In the first phase of my work I got 87%.

November 27, 1942:

Went on a hike. Took code by the blinker system for the first time. Worked three hours scrubbing floors in the barracks.

November 30, 1942:

My final mark for the second phase was 91% giving me an average of 89%.

Thumbing a ride with a very low outside temperature makes this next passage a little surprising. While the USO may be best known for the shows put on for the entertainment of the troops, there are actually USO centers that troops could visit to relax. That appears to be the context of some of Ken's USO mentions.

December 2, 1942:

Skipped breakfast and got up at 9 a.m. Temperature around zero. Thumbed it into St. Louis and went to the U.S.O. for about three hours where I read and played ping pong. Then went to the Wakefields' church at night.

As he wrote, Ken earlier had to help clean the entire barracks because a window sill had dust, so it was surprising that there was not a more serious restriction because of the litter left behind by some of his fellow soldiers, especially with it coming on the year anniversary of Pearl Harbor.

December 7, 1942:

Calisthenics and volleyball in the morning. The Captain inspected the barracks this morning and we were almost restricted for another week because of cigarette butts all over the floor. Saw movies on gas attacks – had a hike using helmets and gas masks. Didn't get much sleep at night because of fellows coming in drunk.

The Wakefields were really good and hospitable to Ken as is evidenced by the next set of notes from letters.

December 23, Wednesday:

Got up at 6:30 a.m. and went into town and spent 5 hours shopping. In the afternoon went to the U.S.O. with Jackie, went to prayer meeting at night. Spent the night at Wakefields'.

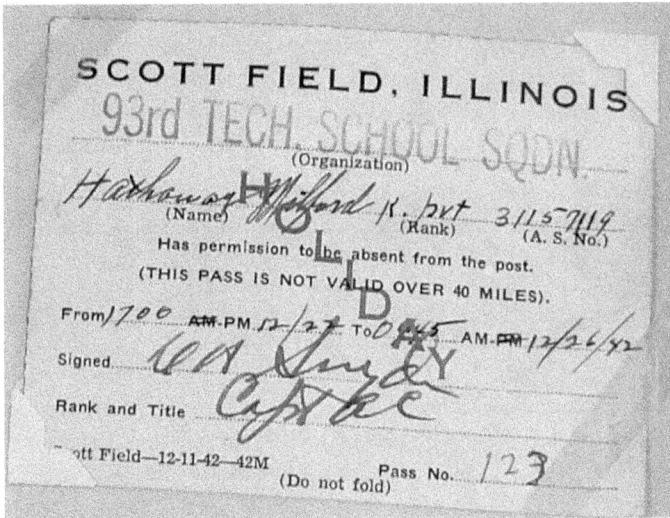

Figure 18. Ken's holiday pass from 12/22/1942 to 12/26/1942.

December 24, 1942, Thursday:

The day before Christmas I went shopping for three hours in the afternoon and church at night. I had seven invitations out to dinner and three to stay overnight. I stayed at the Wakefields'. They gave me a swell pocketbook for Christmas.

December 25, 1942, Friday:

Had my Christmas dinner at the Wakefields'.

1943

Ken had an interesting experience with the local police while he was at Scott Field. Presumably, there were some earlier incidents with other soldiers that led to this type of mistaken identity experience.

January 3, 1943:

I left the field at 4:30 p.m. for St. Louis. I was waiting for a ride when the Belleville Police car drove up, told me to get in and drove me down to the station house. I went in and was told to sit down. After fifteen minutes of sitting there, I inquired as to why I was there. I got no answer so continued sitting there. About five minutes later the Chief of Police called me into his office and began asking all types of questions. He asked me where I lived, how long in the Army, where I was going, what time did I leave the post and so on. After ten minutes of this, I questioned him again as to why I was being held as I had to speak in Young Peoples in St. Louis. I got no answer. Finally two more policemen came in, looked at me, went into a private conference with the chief and then I was questioned again. Finally he asked for my pass and took down my name and Army Serial No. and then let me go. He said he was sorry to bother me but it was a checkup. Went to Katy's house after church.

Ken continued to excel at radio work and continued to visit the St. Louis friends with whom he had connected while stationed at Scott Field. While the military is sometimes like a family, pranks were often more commonplace among the soldiers.

I went for my Gunnery Examination on January 14 at 7:45 a.m. and got through at 9:45 a.m. Forty-five took the exam and only seven passed. I was one of them. Received a mark of 88% in the 5th phase of work. I was the highest in the class with 95% for the last two weeks in radio. I spent Sunday the 24th at church. Ate dinner at Betty Mason's and went to a community sing in the afternoon. There were 800 or 900 there. On Thursday night when I got in to camp I found Grapenuts and corn flakes, newspapers and two bricks in my bed.

His time at Scott Field was starting to wind down. While his stay there was fairly short (4 ½ months), his time was significant because of the relationships that he developed off base. Let me set the stage for the last few letters before he shipped out to the next base.

At the St. Louis church there were a lot of younger folks, and while he was at Scott Field Ken was a regular attendee, or as regular as he could be, of the NYPS (Nazarene Young Peoples Society). Through this program he met several women with whom he developed friendships. One was Betty Mason (a brunette) and the other was a friend of hers, a blonde by the name of Katy Babbs. Ken was attracted to Katy, and this was the start of a romance that lasted the duration of the war, though it had its ups and downs. Betty, a good friend of Katy, ended up being a strong supporter of Ken and of his possible relationship with Katy.

January 30, 1943:

I left school at 6:40 pm and thumbed it into St. Louis. Was I lucky. I got a ride right off and arrived in St. Louis at 8:00 pm. I had supper and went out to a girl's house for the party. We had a swell time, there were 14 of us I believe. We had ice cream and cake for a treat. I walked home with Betty, the brunette, and another fellow and his sister. We started talking in front of Betty's house for almost an hour. I didn't get back to the field until 2:00 AM this morning.

I think I will stay single a little while longer any way. The girls here wanted to find me a wife but there is only one here I would consider and that is Katy. I guess most of them have a pretty good idea that I like her by their remarks.

The end of his time at Scott Field is in sight. He had hopes for a while of being assigned as an instructor and staying at the airbase, but that was not to be.

January 30, 1943:

I was up at 6:00 AM. At 6:30 AM I had breakfast … At 8:00 AM went over to the personal Survey Department. I thought it was to sign up for RL School but instead of that half of us were fingerprinted for RL School and those that passed the gunner's exam were fingerprinted for Aerial Gunnery School, I guess it is pretty certain I am going there, I expect to leave here next Saturday or Sunday. I may even get shipped out before I graduate. Quite a few of my buddies are going to Aerial Gunnery School. We are quite excited about it. I can't be an Instructor anyway as Gunnery has preference. In a way I would like to stay, I may have a chance with the blonde but I have no choice any way in the matter.

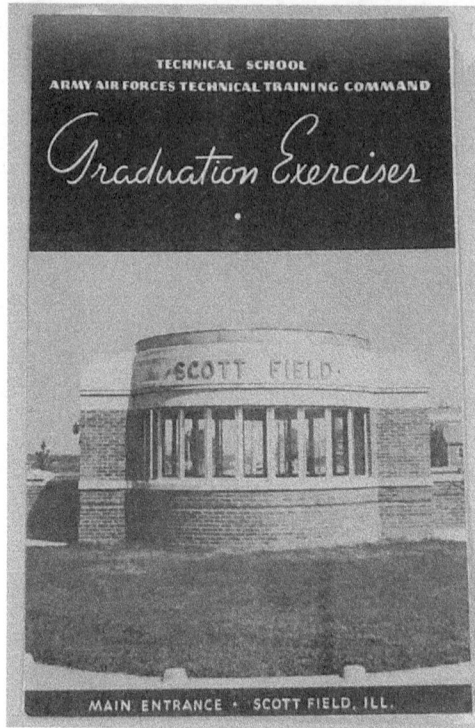

*Figure 19. The graduation program from the Technical School at the
Army Air Forces Technical Training Command at Scott Field.*

It was starting to look like Ken might be assigned to a combat crew since he
was going to aerial gunnery school. He stayed at Scott Field until after the
graduation ceremonies. On February 6, 1943, Private Milfred K. Hathaway
successfully completed the course for radio operators and mechanics and
received his diploma from the Technical School at the Army Air Forces
Technical Training Command.

Chapter 4

Training/Florida

Aerial gunnery school at Buckingham Field in Fort Myers, Florida would be the next destination for Ken. The school name was also the description, since at this next base the soldiers would get more experience with weapons, would get to fly, and then put those two together to train firing the guns while in the planes.

February 8, 1943, Departed Scott Field:

On Monday, the 8th of February, I left Scott Field, Illinois at 9 a.m. and traveled fifty hours by train. We ate dinner in Princeton, Indiana and supper at a hotel in Louisville, Kentucky. When I woke up the next day I was in Chattanooga, Tennessee. When we arrived at Atlanta, Georgia at 10:30 a.m. we got out and did a few exercises and then ate dinner. At 11 p.m. we arrived at Jacksonville, Florida where our train left off one car with fellows headed for R.L. school and after a twenty minute wait we proceeded. R.L. was more or less of a secret school having something to do with radio or radar.

February 9, 1943, Arrived Fort Myers:

At 11 a.m. we arrived at Fort Myers, Florida. This was an *Army Air Forces Flexible Gunnery School* and upon our graduation we would become qualified as aerial gunners. Four days after we arrived at Fort Myers we were called upon to fight a forest fire which covered quite an area. Boy was it hot. This was the first time I had been called upon to do anything like that.

Figure 20. Post card from Fort Myers Florida.

Our five week course at this field was made up mostly of studying machine guns, aircraft recognition, turrets, lectures, movies, and shooting. We did the shooting on the machine gun range, the BB range, the skeet range, and the rifle range.

The training started with more shooting practice. Ken was improving and even received a rank of marksmanship.

On February 16 I scored 28 out of a possible 50 points on the shooting range. Twenty-six was passing. The next day I scored 35 out of 50 which qualified me for marksmanship. Some days I wasn't even able to pass. It all depended on the wind. For two days in a row I scored only 12 and 14 points respectively. On my second Sunday in Fort Myers I went to church on the post in the morning and in the afternoon went into the city. I stayed in the city for church at night and there were about twenty-five out. On the skeet range I had quite a bit of trouble. We had to shoot little discs. Some days I got as little as two hits out of fifteen shots. On other days I would get nine out of twenty or ten out of fifteen shots. It seemed as though the harder the range the more points I could score. For example on the Moving Base Range where we rode on the back of a truck and fired at moving discs, two would come out of a little house at the same time, one on each side and I would hit both of them before they fell down. This helped to pull up my average. On the Jeep Range where we fired 50 and 30 caliber machine guns I got 9 hits in 50 shots on the 50 caliber and 30 hits in 130 shots on the 30 caliber.

The training continued with more gunnery practice, repair, and aircraft identification. The aircraft identification covered both theaters of the war since air corps soldiers were being sent both to Europe and to the Pacific.

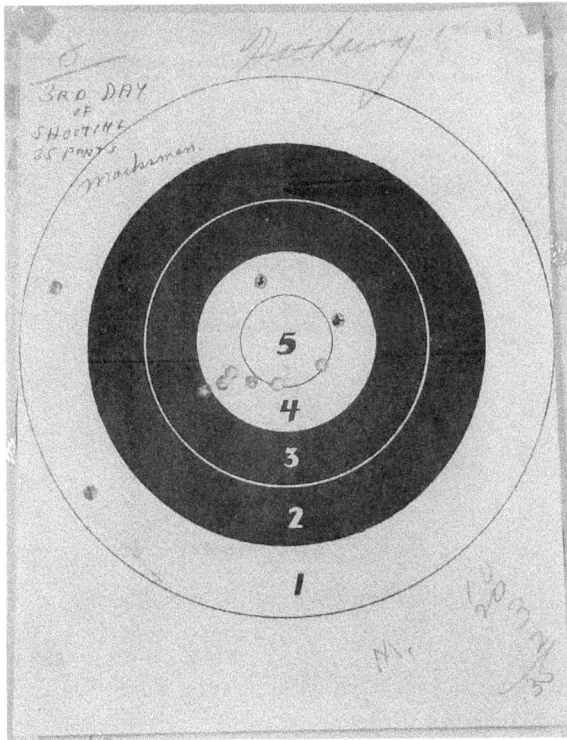

Figure 21. Ken's target where he scored marksman.

February 23, 1943:

I don't know how they figure out our marks. I know you have to get 26 points out of 50 to qualify. I qualified in two out of 5 days which passes me. I was a marksman for that day only. When I get to my next post if my shooting is good I may have a chance to get a medal I don't know for sure. They figure it day by day here on the marksmanship basis and your final mark is figured on the average of the class I believe.

Two weeks from tomorrow we start flying and firing machine guns in the air at a target towed by another plane. Three weeks from tomorrow I graduate if I pass and will have my wings and Staff Sergeant rating. I am certainly studying hard as I want them bad.

Wednesday we had a lousy breakfast as usual and drilled. In school in the morning we had plane recognition. German planes. How to recognize them by their different wing, tail, fuselage etc. We have 30 planes altogether and this is one of the hardest parts of the course. We also had movies for one hour on how to recognize the Japanese planes and then we went to the Malfunction Range, which I explained previously. Boy do the 50 caliber machine guns make an awful noise. In afternoon we had lectures on how to sight. If plane is moving fast how to figure out how far ahead of it to shoot etc. We also had B.B. shooting. It was very hot out all day. We had a test on sighting, I got 100%.

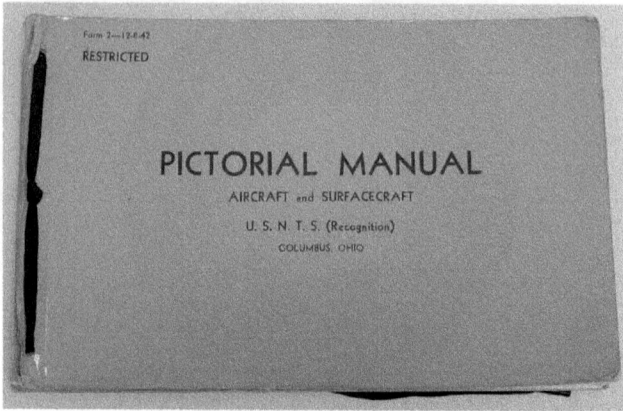

Figure 22. Restricted Pictorial Manual for Aircraft Identification.

Thursday – In morning we had more planes to recognize, Japanese, Russian and Italian. Out to the Malfunction Range we had our test. We had ten machine guns with something wrong with them. Some wouldn't fire, some would fire one cartridge and stop. We had two minutes to find out the trouble. I got at least 9 of them right. It was fun but you had to be on your toes and spot the trouble immediately. In afternoon we had lectures on sighting and movies for an hour on sighting. We also had more airplanes to recognize, British planes. It was the hottest day yet here. The temperature was well over 80.

Well we had to go to night school for a lecture on turrets. If you have ever noticed the glass dome on top of planes with guns sticking out, or on the bottom of bombers. We are studying how to work one of them. Each one has two 50 caliber machine guns in it. I am lucky the one I am studying is only in the B-17E or B-17F the largest bomber we make or the Flying Fortress. That means I may be lucky enough when I leave here to be stationed as radio operator and machine gunner in the largest bomber we have, I hope I make it.

Ken really wanted to be on a B-17, so this training gave him hope. He wanted to be part of a crew on the largest bomber; in a sense that part was to come true.

February 23, 1943:

Friday – today – This morning we had a two hour lecture on the turret on the top of the plane. We also went inside one, not in a plane, just in a building, and learned how to manipulate the controls. In the afternoon we had a two hour lecture on the turret on the bottom of the plane, it is a little different from the top one, it is just like a ball. We then had our final test on sighting. I got at least 90% maybe higher. … We have to go to school again tonight for a review on Aircraft recognition. We have our big test on that in a couple of days. I don't know how long school will last tonight probably two hours. That makes three nights this week to school. They certainly rush you around here.

March 13, 1943:

We were almost through our course now and would soon become flyers and receive our wings. On Saturday, March 13, we received flying instructions such as how to put on our life belt and parachute, how to pull the rip cord, how to inflate the life belt and signals used in flying. Then we ran the Burma Road with the temperature over 85 degrees. We were now ready for our first flight. On March 15 the great day came.

Ken had never flown in a plane before, so the flight was going to be a new experience and very exciting.

March 15, 1943:

Changing into my flying clothes I reported at the field ready to fly. When my turn came I got my ammunition and climbed into the rear cockpit of the AT-6, I fastened the gunner's belt which comes up from the floor and goes around your parachute strap. I finally got all settled and had 100 rounds to fire as practice rounds. We taxied out on to the runway and finally headed for the takeoff. What a thrill! We climbed up to 1600 feet and were going around 160 miles an hour. We headed down to the Gulf of Mexico and fired my shots into the water just to get the feel of things. We then headed back and landed. By the time we got back to the field and landed they had started on regular missions. We never had any dinner as due to getting a late start and our first practice mission coming at noontime we didn't eat. Was I hungry. I hung around and at 5:00 PM received orders I was to take off on my first regular mission. I got my helmet and goggles and my gear, took my gun partially apart and checked it to be sure it was all right. I then got 200 rounds of ammunition and reported to plane #511. We roared down the runway and soon climbed to 4,000 feet at 170 miles per hour. We finally got out over the gulf and the pilot wiggled the wings to signal me to load the guns. I loaded the gun and then he wiggled the wings again to signal me to start firing. I fired at a target towed by another plane. When we fire we undo our safety belt and stand up in the plane being held in by our gunner's belt which comes up through the floor to our parachute. I don't know how many shots hit the target but very few shots did hit it. It was plenty windy and hard to hold the gun still. We had to change ammunition cans as each can holds 100 rounds. In changing ammunition cans the wind almost took it out of my hands. It certainly is a thrill riding way up there. We got through at 6 p.m.

Figure 23. The AT-6 was also known as the SNJ in Naval circles. This was the plane on which the aerial shooting training took place. This is a page from the Pictorial Manual mentioned in Figure 22.

March 16, 1943:

The next day I reported to the airfield at 7:30 a.m. We took off at 11 a.m. and went to around 5,000 feet at 200 miles an hour. When we got out over the gulf the pilot wiggled the wings as a signal to load the gun. I loaded it and sat down. He then gave the signal to fire. I got 150 out of the 200 rounds fired when my gun jammed. I worked for five minutes trying to fix it and then gave up. My ejector hook was broken. I raised my fist as a signal for the pilot to head back to the field and upon our arrival I reported the trouble. At 4:30 p.m. I went up again, and this time I had no trouble firing my 200 rounds. On the 17th we did not fly. We were privileged to see a bomber pilot receive the Distinguished Service Cross for extraordinary heroism in sinking a German submarine and capturing its crew.

On Thursday I reported at the airfield at 7 a.m. It was very foggy. At 1 p.m. I went up and had no trouble firing my 200 rounds at the target. As soon as I landed I was ordered up again. This time I fired 160 rounds and my gun stopped again. I had another broken ejector hook. I signaled the pilot that my gun wouldn't work. We were up at 3,000 feet. When he saw my signal he put the plane into a slide slip and then into a dive. I could see the water getting nearer and nearer. With less than 100 feet to spare he pulled out of the dive. We went along just over the gulf and then all at once he went straight up to about 1,500 feet. It sure was a thrill.

It seems as though I always had trouble when I went up and for that reason I had to make extra trips to get in the required amount of shooting from a plane. I went up on Friday with 300 rounds and only fired 1 round. My charging handle came loose. I just got back when I was told to report to plane 706 to go up again. After waiting a half hour the pilot told me that the machine gun mounting was broken, I reported back to the dispatcher and went to the PX to get a bite to eat as this was the third day without dinner. I was eating a ham sandwich when a fellow came in and called #113 which was my number. I got my ammunition and went over to the plane. Then for the last time I took off of the runway at Buckingham Air Field and after a lot of trouble I finally fired all my rounds. I cut the palm of my hand open by hand charging it so much. I finished my eighth trip in the air at Fort Myers at 1:30 p.m.

Sadly, lives were not only lost during combat, but throughout his training there were several times when Ken reported sad news about some soldiers losing their lives in training accidents. Despite all the safety precautions, at times the training was dangerous and occasionally soldiers did not survive those accidents. I suspect this was more common in the Air Corps than in other branches of the military because of the challenges of not only training soldiers to fly, but also to fight in the air.

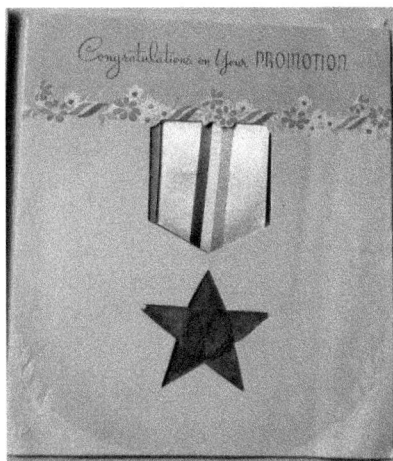

Figure 24. A promotion card Ken received.

A friend of mine was an infant when he lost his father on a training mission during World War II. His father never saw combat, but served his country faithfully. The losses that occur during war and combat are significant and worthy of remembrance, but it is easy to forget that lives were also lost in training. These losses are not commemorated in the same way we honor other wartime loses, but these are still soldiers who died for their country. For example, earlier in March, Ken wrote:

March 15, 1943:

I do have some bad news though and as you will probably read about it in the paper thought I had better mention it. Just before I went up on my second mission I heard that one of the planes went into a power dive at 3,000 feet never pulling out of it. I saw the tail of the plane sticking out of the water. Both the pilot and gunner were killed. The gunner was in our squadron and a couple of barracks from mine. They say it was his fault as he stepped on the control cables in the cockpit and thereby caused the pilot to lose control of the plane. All the pilots here are experts and have many flying hours to their credit. In fact I think this is the first accident of its kind here. I wouldn't worry about it, it will probably not happen again here. It hasn't bothered anybody we all want to go up again tomorrow.

Promotions are always a proud time for a soldier and Ken was no different. In his letter to his brother Dud from March 21, his promotion was the first thing he mentioned.

March 21, 1943:

I received a letter from you today and as once again I can't get into town for any church service I thought I would drop a line. This will be my last letter as Private Hathaway. Will write the next time as Sergeant Hathaway.

There were good days and bad days as far as firing practice went. On a good day, Ken made marksmanship scores, on other days he barely scored at all, but overall he did enough to pass.

March 21, 1943:

I sure do wish I had had more shooting practice at home. We got our marks in our air to air firing and once again I just squeezed by. I've got to get on the ball if I expect to bring down any planes.

Sergeant Milfred K. Hathaway Jr., son of Mr. and Mrs. M. K. Hathaway of 108 Pierce Street, has been graduated from the Army Air Forces Flexible Gunnery School at Fort Myers, Fla. Sergeant Hathaway is also a graduate of radio operators school.

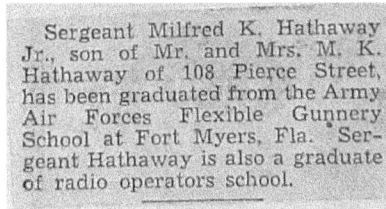

Figure 25. Graduation announcement in newspaper.

Soldiers were always trying to figure out where they would be going next, in part so they could at least let their family and friends know.

March 21, 1943:

I have an idea I may be shipped to Salt Lake City, Utah. I would like to get near home or at least near St. Louis, but of course we have to be satisfied with where they do send us.

I will write again Tuesday if not tomorrow and will write the day I ship out if I have time. If you suddenly don't hear from me for a week you will know I have been shipped out.

At this point Ken was able to get some passes, but unlike the previous location he did not talk a lot about non-military activities. It might have been a combination of being so busy, but also they were only at Fort Myers for a short time, a little over two months, and as such did not have as much opportunity to develop relationships like he did while in Illinois. Instead, he was often writing about getting new equipment and military insignias.

March 21, 1943:

Last night I had a pass to go into town but decided to go in today instead so I turned my pass back in. I wish I hadn't now. I could have got my wings and stripes etc. As luck would have it our pass today is only good until 4:00 PM so there was no sense in going in town. This morning I had an examination for insurance, I took out $5,000 more and that took three hours. The reason our pass was only good until 4:00 PM is that two generals are visiting the field tomorrow and at 4:00 PM we have to clean our entire squadron from one end to the other. It is now 1:00 PM and we will have to get to work pretty soon.

Tomorrow morning we get our flying equipment, Boy what equipment, I wish you could see it. It certainly looks swell. We graduate at 4:00 PM tomorrow. If I can get a pass I am going into town and get my stripes. They give us a combat crew wings at graduation but I want to also buy a gunners wings.

Ken was very close to all of his family, but he did seem especially close to his youngest brother, Dud. Maybe that is a biased view since most of the letters used for this book were letters he sent to Dud, but he was always going into military details and answering questions when he was writing Dud.

Figure 26. Ken (right) and his youngest brother Dud.

March 22, 1943:

This is the first letter I have written as a Sergeant and thought I would address it to you.

This morning we received our flying equipment and you should see it. What equipment. We have a winter fur lined helmet, a fur lined flying suit and fur lined flying boots, a summer flying helmet and suit, a pair of sun glasses costing $20, a pair of leather gloves, a leather jacket, two sweaters, coveralls, oxygen mask, a Mae West or water life belt and our parachute. You ought to see our traveling bags I will bring it home when I come on furlough.

Well this afternoon I graduated and have been sewing on my stripes. I received my wings and have them on now. It certainly was a thrill to receive them. We didn't get a diploma but I am enclosing a graduation paper, also a paper we had to have to fly last week and a dentist slip as a souvenir from Scott Field.

I certainly would like to be a pilot and probably will make application at my next field. It would mean 8 months longer in this country. I didn't feel nervous going up but did feel excited. I didn't even know I had left the ground.

I just heard they had Gunners wings in the PX and I did a 100 yd dash over there, I got to within 5 of the counter and they were all sold out. They certainly go fast. We are given at graduation the Combat Crew Wings. Most of us like the Gunners Wings a little better. They are a little more fancier.

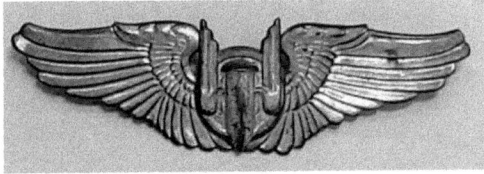

Figure 27. The highly sought-after gunner's wings.

I don't know whether I told you or not but we had a fellow go crazy here in the barracks the second week of school. They have a whole building of them here. It really is too bad.

There isn't much news to write about as I have been writing every day. I doubt if I will write again until the day I ship out. I expect to leave here around Thurs. or Friday at the latest.

Well I guess I will close. I have some more stripes to sew on and Air Corps emblems.

The time to ship out again was fast approaching. In the next letter to his younger brother Dud, Ken shared a surprising amount of information on various war planes which was not censored.

March 27, 1943, Fort Myers FL:

Half of our crowd shipped out today to various schools, of course we that are waiting have been to school and are waiting to be shipped out to our Operational training Units.

I am sending 25 photographs of planes I thought you might like. The one on top is the B-17E, This is the kind I hope I fly in. Just underneath the star you can see the gun sticking out of the lower turret.

The next on, B-26 is a medium bomber and some of the fellows that were shipped out today are going to a B-26 outfit. You can see the top turret good in this one.

Figure 28. Post card showing P-39 Airacobras.

The next is an AT-6. This is the plane I flew in on my trips here. You can see the glass covered canopy for the pilot and gunner. The back part where the gunner sits was open when I went up for shooting purposes.

The next one, the B-19, they are still experimenting with.

I don't know a lot of them. The P-39 is one of our best fighters, also the P-36, P-40, Air cobra, P-38 and P-51.

The B-25 is another of our large bombers, The A-20A and A24 are two seater dive bombers or light bombers.

Well there is no news around here. I expect to leave tomorrow. I hope so, I am all packed and all we do is hang around all day. I would rather be doing something.

While training at Fort Myers, Ken completed 8 trips in the air and the soldiers called these flights missions because they were intended to prepare them for the real missions they would face.

Chapter 5

Training/Idaho

Salt Lake City, Utah

The next base would be the Sub Air Base #1 in Salt Lake City, Utah, but it was really just a stop of a couple of days for assignment before moving on to another location. On the trip to Salt Lake City, they stopped in St. Louis and Ken was able to call some of those who he had gotten to know when he was stationed at Scott Field. There was no mention of trying to contact Katy, which is a bit surprising. They also stopped in Kansas City which was the location of the headquarters of the Church of the Nazarene.

March 28, 1943, Departed Fort Myers:

On the afternoon of March 27 I left Fort Myers for Salt lake City, Utah. We arrived in Jacksonville, Florida at 7 a.m. Sunday and so I went to the Nazarene Church there. After church I was invited out to dinner and had chicken. At 9 p.m. I left Jacksonville and by noon the next day I arrived in Birmingham Alabama (3/30). Upon my arrival at St. Louis I had one hour to spend so I called Mrs. Wakefield and Mrs. O'Bannon. At 6 p.m. we arrived at Kansas City, Missouri. Here we had five hours to ourselves. I tried to locate the pastor of the Nazarene Church but he was at a convention. By the help of some members of the church I met a fellow who works in the publishing house. He took me through the building and then back to the station. By this time most of the fellows were pretty drunk. The next thing we knew there were ten M.P.'s around us. One fellow was thrown in jail and seven others were almost. One fellow was hit by a club and his eye was closed the next morning. When I woke up on Wednesday we were in Nebraska (3/31). While we were stopped in Cheyenne, Wyoming, I met the Nazarene minister.

April 1, 1943, Arrived Salt Lake City:

At noontime on April 1 we reached Salt Lake City.

In the morning we had our processing which included a physical examination etc. I was assigned to the 2nd Air Corp, composed entirely of heavy bombardment. I stayed in Salt Lake City for a little over a week during which time I did practically nothing. I visited the minister one night and went to church another night. The church was the First Church of the Nazarene at 6th East and 5th South.

Since Ken was assigned to the 2nd Air Corps, it was pretty much guaranteed that he would be involved with heavy bombers in some capacity.

April 3, 1943, postcard:

Well I think I am getting my wish. I believe I will get shipped out as a B-17 outfit. Will be west of the Mississippi however but hope I am near St. Louis. Am having a swell time traveling. Wish I could get home. Will try at my next post as that will be my permanent post while in the U.S.A.

Around this time Ken received word that his sister Marjorie was in the hospital. This may have been when she was diagnosed with diabetes, which would have a huge impact on the rest of her life, including eventually leading to her going blind. In a card labeled April 1943 Marjorie talked about how the injection had affected her eyes and that she had trouble seeing, but that it should go away.

Boise, Idaho

Ken's arrival in Boise, ID was interesting in that he was able to immediately get a pass and go to church. Attending church services were always a priority for Ken.

April 10, 1943, Departed Salt Lake City:

We left Salt Lake City at 9 p.m. April 10 and were given a siren escort by the M.P.'s down to the station. We arrived at Gowen Field, Boise Idaho at 2 p.m. Sunday (4/11). I immediately got a pass and went to the First Church of the Nazarene, 1501 Franklin Street, Boise Idaho. Fred W. Fetters was the pastor. They were having a revival meeting at the church and we had a good service.

There were many simple, non-military projects to which the soldiers sometimes were assigned and completed. Ken also received his yellow fever shot that he had mentioned earlier, but said nothing about getting sick afterwards.

April 12, 1943, letter:

This morning we had detail work. We were putting in posts and stringing wire around the squadron. This afternoon we had our final big physical qualifying us for flying. One fellow was disqualified and 7 others grounded temporarily. I have finished my physical except for my eye test. If you're grounded you can get a furlough otherwise you can't, we will only be here around a month. We get 60 hours of flying here. We then go to another state for our second phase or 30 more hours of flying and finally to another state for 30 more hours. Three phases in all. We are supposed to get a furlough after our third phase as we are then subject to overseas call. Here's hoping I get one. That would be in about three months. I had three shots this morning on one arm. A shot for Yellow Fever, one for Typhus and one for Cholera. My arm was sore for a while. Three in one arm at one time is plenty.

Ken wrote about another tragic training accident, this time involving multiple planes.

April 13, 1943:

I was sleeping at 8:30 a.m. when all of a sudden I heard an awful crash then an explosion and sirens. I jumped out of bed and ran over to the field about one-fifth of a mile away. Ambulances were coming in all directions and also fire engines. Three of our huge B-17's or Flying Fortresses had crashed. One plane only had its wing smashed, the other two were burning. One was cut in half. It was a terrible mess. Latest reports are that five were killed and twelve in the hospital. I saw three taken in the ambulance myself. One fellow had his arm all torn up and was lying on the ground waiting for the ambulance. He had walked out of the plane but fell on the ground after a few steps. A fellow who was sleeping across from me pulled the co-pilot out of one ship. He was covered in blood and dead. The pilot of this plane was also dead. The planes had crashed into the carpenter's shop and demolished it. It just missed the orderly room. At 10:30 a.m. the planes were still burning. The fellow across from me came in later in the day with a bandaged eye. He got smoke and a piece of steel in his eye. He had saved one pilot and co-pilot I believe.

Ken mentioned the three phases of flight training, but did not go into detail as to what the phases were other than the flying hours, and they were going to be doing lots of flying in Idaho.

April 12, 1943:

Expect to start flying this week. Thought I would be in a B-17 but may be put in a B-24 called the Liberator, a 4 motor heavy bomber. ... We fly

4 hours at a time and sometimes go up 12 hours in a day or more. Sometimes midnight to 4:00 AM or anytime. We are on 24 hr duty, 7 days a week. I like it here. The field is swell and food good. Have been made C.G. in my barracks until I start flying. Am on duty from 4:00 PM to midnight. Have to keep fire going and wake up those who fly around midnight.

Ken did get assigned to a crew, though he did not elaborate yet on his crew mates.

April 15, 1943:

At night I found out I was assigned to crew 34A. I knew one of the fellows. The pilot comes from Ohio, the bombardier from New Mexico, the 1st Radio Operator and two others from New York.

There were a significant number of little issues that often occurred during training flights.

April 16, 1943:

Our plane wasn't ready so we went all through a B-17F. At 3 P.M. our ship was ready and we took off. As our pilot was new we were to make practice landings. We circled the field, came in and he made a perfect landing. We took off again and circled the field and came in again. This time the shearing pin in the tail wheel let go and it felt as though we had a flat tire. We bounced along for 100 feet or so. Left the field at 4:15 P.M.

Even those in the Air Corps might get air sick on occasion. It could be a problem if it persisted, but it was more understandable while the crews still adjusting to flying.

April 19, 1943:

After waiting since midnight went to bed because no plane came in. Got 3 hours sleep and reported to the ready room at 7:30 A.M. as I was to fly from 8:00 A.M. until noon. Because of threatening weather we didn't fly until 11:00 A.M. I had my first taste of air sickness. About a half hour before I came down with my stomach starting to feel woozy and the next thing I knew I was throwing up. It was very bumpy in the air. We landed at 12:15 P.M. and I skipped dinner. Went to radio school from 1:00 P.M. to 5:00 P.M. Skipped a lecture at 5:15 P.M. Weather cold and rainy, Went to bed at 8:00 P.M.

I'm not sure how much of this next passage is part of their training, verses pilot choice. It makes sense that the crews should be exposed to a variety of mid-air maneuvers, and flying in formation was also to be expected, but stunt flying was probably not typical.

April 24, 1943:

12:01 A.M. to 4:00 A.M. flying. Roughest it has ever been. Was sick the last hour and threw up. Got two hours sleep and then flew from 7:30 A.M. to 12:30 P.M. This time I didn't get sick. It was a bombing run. I took pictures with a large camera through a two foot square hole in the floor. When I saw the puff of smoke indicating the bomb hitting the ground I snapped the picture. On the way back our pilot did a half hour of stunt flying. What a thrill and what a feeling. He went into a dive and one of the fellows who was sitting on the floor of the radio compartment was lifted about a foot into the air where he stayed for a few seconds. I was sitting in the chair and a radio book came off the shelf and floated right toward me. I tried to push it down but it came right up. I was lifted about 4 inches off the chair and my right leg which was in the aisle went right up in the air. The pilot then went straight up in the air and then we couldn't move. We couldn't even lift our leg off the floor. As I looked out of my window the sky was where the ground should be and vice versa. We also flew in formation for about an hour with a plane on each side nearly touching wings. Skipped three classes in the afternoon. Had my name taken by the Lieutenant because my floor was dirty.

It is not clear what the stunt flying entailed. At one point, Ken's letter almost seems to imply that the pilot flew the B-24 inverted. Whether or not a B-24 could be flown inverted is debatable. Another possible option is that the plane was flying with the wings vertical so that out one window there was nothing but sky and out the opposite window there was nothing but ground. Whatever the stunt flying was, it seemed to make an impression on Ken.

While Ken had been part of the crew, the policy changed in regards to radio operators, so the official assignment of a radio operator to a crew was not going to happen until the radio operator had passed all the needed coursework and was checked out on all the equipment.

April 27, 1943:

I am no longer with my crew. Effective at midnight last night Radio Operators are not assigned to a crew until they have been checked on all the radio equipment. We will still fly but will go up with different crews each time. As soon as we have passed all the tests we are assigned to a crew here for one week solid flying with them then we move to our next base.

We are still flying on the Flying Fortress but have quite a few Liberators in here now. If I can't get out soon I will probably go on the Liberator. It is a bigger plane, carries more of a bomb load but I don't think is as well protected.

Another unusual assignment, washing a B-17!

April 27, 1943:

Monday I was up at 6:00 AM I went to Radio school from 7:00 AM to 11:00 AM. I was supposed to fly from 12:00 noon until 4:00 PM as almost all the planes were grounded for inspection we didn't fly. Instead we had to wash a B-17. I never thought they were so big until I had to wash one. We spent about two hours on the plane. At 8:00 PM I reported to flying again and once more didn't fly. I hung around until 10:00 PM and quit.

More flying and training filled the following letters Ken wrote and Dud saved.

April 27, 1943:

This morning I got up at 6:30 AM. I was supposed to fly from 8:00 AM until noontime. As most of the planes were still grounded we didn't go up. My regular crew has been 34A. I was supposed to go up with crew 30A this morning. Now instead of hanging around or washing planes when we don't fly we have to go to Radio School. I got out of school at 11:00 AM. At 12:30 PM this afternoon we had to have shots again. I had two in my left arm, one for Typhus and a booster or stimulus for tetanus. It hurt plenty for a while but is okay now. After getting my shots I had my oxygen mask adjusted as this morning if we had gone up we would have been up at 20,000 feet and had to use it.

Well I went up again this afternoon for four hours 4:00 PM to 8:00 PM. Went on a gunnery mission, I did the duties of first radio operator and didn't fire any guns. The Armor Gunner and Engineer fired the guns.

All the fellows that were in my car were radio operators but in the train we had medical men and mechanics and some others I believe. There are a few Staff Sergeants here but they graduated from gunnery school before the new ruling went into effect. Nobody can get ratings here. When you leave here if you go as 1st Radio Operator you make Staff Sergeant. I have as good a chance as anyone of making Tech Sergeant. I am flying at present only in Flying Fortress. Our bombers have names like Jinx, Susie, etc. but I go up in a different one most of the time so I never pay attention to its name.

At present our flights only cover the state of Idaho although we do go to Oregon on some gunnery missions. I haven't been yet. In our third phase in two months we go on cross country flights and then we will probably go from coast to coast.

I got my Gunners wings. They don't have any for sale here but one of the fellows was hard up for money and sold me his for $2.00.

P.S. Will Explain the bomber in my next letter if I can.

Katy, the girl from St. Louis in whom Ken was interested, had a boyfriend. There were several times when Ken would state in his letters where he felt he stood in comparison to her boyfriend.

April 27, 1943:

I stand high with Katy but not as high as her boyfriend. I am making progress though. Would know more if I could see her again.

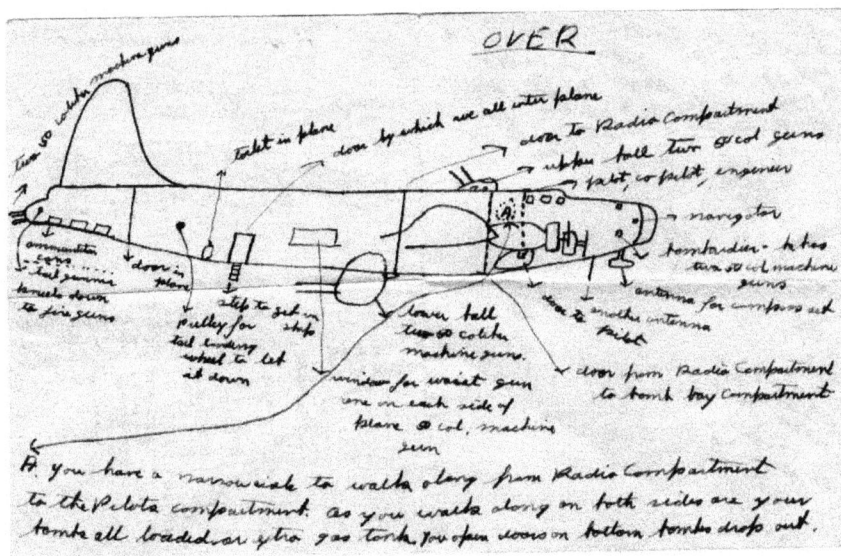

Figure 29. Ken's drawing of the B-17 identifying everything for his younger brother Dud.

Ken made several diagrams of his planes to share with his younger brother.

April 30, 1943:

Compartment on the other side of the paper. I am a rotten drawer as you can see.

Ken was excelling as a radio operator.

April 30, 1943:

This morning I got up at 7:00 AM. I flew from 9:00 AM to 11:00 AM. We were supposed to have an Instructor Radio fellow go up but there wasn't any room as we had 12 going up and there were only 12 parachutes. He asked me if I thought I could handle the Radio alone as I was to be 1st Radio Operator. I told him I could and did a good job of it. He is going to recommend that when I go up here I go up as 1st Radio Operator. I went to school from 1:00 PM to 3:00 PM and checked out

OK on the Liaison Radio Set in school. I hope to check out on the Command Radio Set tomorrow and the Compass Monday, then I can be assigned to my regular crew. I flew again from 4:00 PM to 8:00 PM as 1st radio operator. I did a good job getting weather reports and calling the control. It is a lot of fun. I hope to make permanent 1st Radio Operator.

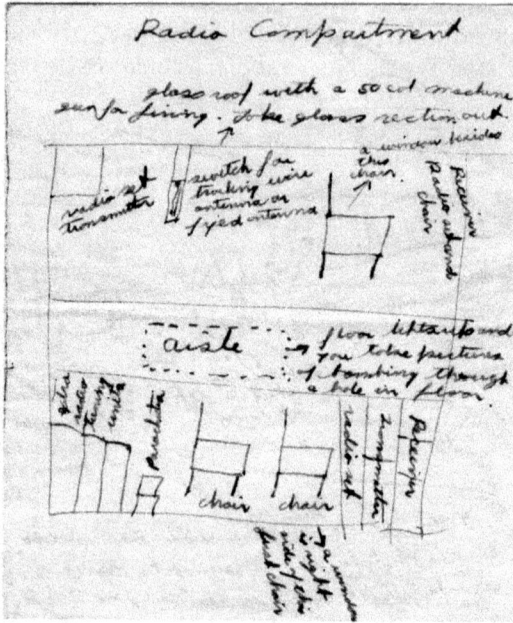

Figure 30. Ken's drawing of the Radio Compartment for the B-17.

There were several times when Ken either listened to rumors, or simply slept too long and got into hot water because of not doing something that he was supposed to have done. As he wrote, it always paid to make sure to get the official word on any changes of plans.

May 3, 1943:

At 4:00 A.M. we got in the plane and were already to fly when word came one of our planes crashed in the mountains and all planes were grounded. My pilot told me I could go back to the barracks so I did. At 7:30 A.M. the sergeant woke me up and told me the Officer of the Day wanted to see me. I knew immediately I was in trouble. Sure enough I was threatened with everything in the book because I didn't stand by this morning. He threatened to make me stand at attention for two hours, march five hours on the ramp with a pack on my back and report to him every two hours for 24 hours. I got out of it with no punishment.

May 6, 1943:

Was dismissed at 2:00 A.M. after waiting since midnight to fly. Woke up at 8:00 A.M. and was two hours late for school and the sgt. was sore. If he had turned my name in I would have been busted to a private.

The amount of communication that took place between Katy and members of Ken's family, especially his sister Marge, is interesting:

May 10, 1943:

Glad to hear Katy sent her (Marjorie) a card (probably because of her hospitalization) and note. I sent Katy a birthday card and a pillow top. Her birthday is May 14th. She will be 21 years old.

At the same time, he was friends and corresponded with several girls, but he always tried to be honest and forthright in his communications about relationships.

May 10, 1943:

I sent Muriel a pillow top Saturday, One of the reasons I have hesitated is the wording on it. I don't want to get any more serious than it is although she is a swell girl. I just don't feel like getting so serious especially seeing eventually I will no doubt be going across.

There were a lot of training accidents involving the aircraft, not unexpected with pilots and crew with little flying experience. Ken tried to be transparent and let the family know about them most of the time, but he also tried to balance that with not wanting them to worry any more than necessary. Evidently, there was one accident he didn't write home about, but the clipping in Figure 31 is the article that his family saw in the local paper.

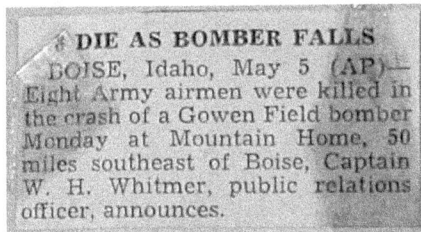

DIE AS BOMBER FALLS

BOISE, Idaho, May 5 (AP)— Eight Army airmen were killed in the crash of a Gowen Field bomber Monday at Mountain Home, 50 miles southeast of Boise, Captain W. H. Whitmer, public relations officer, announces.

Figure 31. Short newspaper article on a bomber training accident.

May 10, 1943:

I meant to tell you about the crash and then I decided not to. It seems when I write about them you don't read about them and then I figure if I don't write you won't worry. If I don't write you read about them in the paper. We have certainly had tough luck here in the last few weeks, and as we have had three bad accidents and all things come in threes I hope it is the end of them for a while.

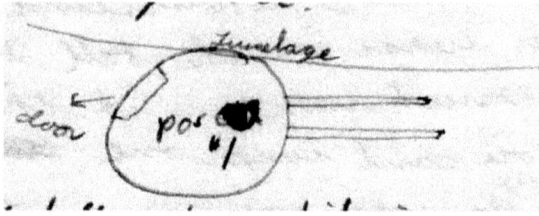

Figure 32. Ken's drawing of the ball turret, position 1.

Ken tried to explain to his younger brother as many details as he could about the operations of various parts of the plane. Below he explained about the plane's lower turret, how to get in and out of it and how it worked.

May 10, 1943:

On the question of the lower turret. The only way you get into the lower turret is through the plane. You hand crank it around inside the plane until the door comes up. You then get into it and operate it by electrical power. Position of ball when ship is on the ground. Guns pointing toward tail. You can't turn the ball around on the ground because the guns will hit the ground so you have to wait until the plane gets into the air then you turn the ball around until it is like this (Figure 33). You climb in and bring the ball around to Pos #1 to operate if firing straight ahead. When you finish you bring the ball into Pos #2 again and get out. Then you hand crank it to Pos #1 and the plane is ready to land.

Figure 33. Ken's drawing of the ball turret, position 2.

At present you wear no parachute when in the lower ball so in order to bail out you would have to bring the ball around into position and climb into the plane and get your parachute. They are making a parachute so I understand which you can wear in the ball. There isn't much room in it that is why you can't wear one. If you do wear one you just open the door and fall out backwards.

We never wear our parachute in the plane and just have one near us.

Ken went on to say that much of the rest of the crew didn't wear parachutes in the plane, but they made sure to have one nearby that they could grab in case of trouble. Ken also tried to explain who might be manning which guns.

May 10, 1943:

On the guns, the 2nd armorer is in the tail gun position, The 1st armorer is the waist position on one side and the 2nd engineer on a waist gun the other side, 1st engineer is in the upper turret, 2nd radio man is ball turret and 1st radio man has a machine gun in the radio room which only fires up into the air through the roof. The bombardier also has two guns in the front of the ship. Of course all these positions aren't exact because the 2nd armorer might be better fitted for the ball turret than the radio man especially if he is a short fellow. I have heard recently that the 2nd radio man doesn't go in the ball turret but handles a waist gun now so none of these positions are exact, however it is the general idea now. 1st radio operator during combat would be in the Radio room handling the radio room gun.

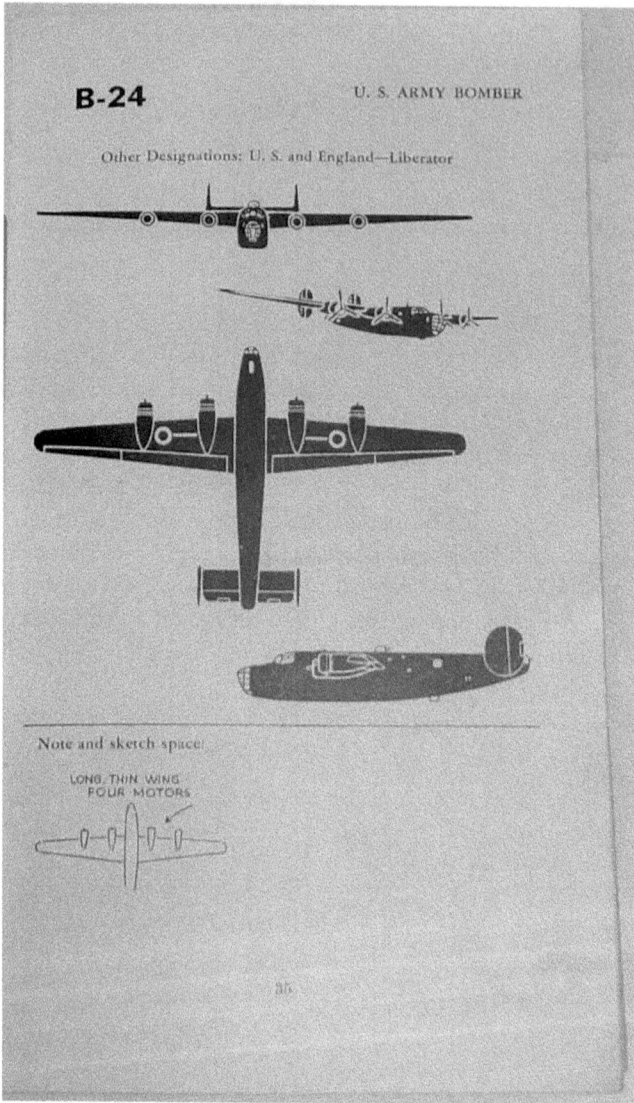

Figure 34. B-24 identification information from the Identification of Aircraft booklet.

Ken did not live up to the next boast; at least there is no evidence of him shooting down an enemy plane.

May 10, 1943:

Thanks for the compliment on being the best radio gunner and you can be sure when I get across I will bring down more than one plane if at all possible.

More and More B-24s were arriving and the inevitable was about to happen.

May 10, 1943:

Well church let out at 9:30PM and I got back to the field around 11:00 PM. As I went by the ramp I noticed quite a few B-24s but didn't think much about it.

Figure 35. B-24s from the Pictorial Manual for Aircraft from Figure 22.

I got up this morning at 6:30 and went to school. There I heard the bad news. Our squadron is completely a B-24 squadron now. The only squadron on the field. They kept 36 radio operators and sent the rest to other squadrons of B-17. I was one of the ones kept for the B-24 because I had had so much flying time in the air. I felt kind of bad at first but figure maybe it is for the best. We have been told we will all be out of here by the end of this month. As you know this is the Liberator our biggest and heaviest bomber. It has four motors and is a twin tail job. It is about 50 miles an hour faster than the B-17 and carries about 4000 more pounds of bombs. It isn't as heavily armored as the B-17 or as heavily plated but I understand they are adding more guns to it.

I still like the Flying Fortress better but they claim the B-24 is a better ship. I believe the largest bomber in the world at present is the Lancaster, Britain's heavy bomber is bigger. If I get a good picture of the B-24 will send it to you. It is too bad but at least it is still a heavy bomber. They claim they have cut the B-17 production and that they were concentrating on production of the B-29 which will be the largest bomber in the world carrying 15 tons, 30,000 lbs. of bombs.

I haven't been up in a B-24 yet but will let you know how it is. Will probably go up tomorrow or Wednesday. There will be no more night flying here at least from 8:00 PM to 4:00 AM so I will be getting more sleep.

There is a slight chance I may get shipped further East by being in a B-24 than a B-17 as those going out in B-17 have been getting shipped to Walla Walla Washington, Wendover Field Utah, or Casper Wyoming. Let's hope it is for the best anyways. It is a good plane and probably the only reason I like the B-17 better is because of the name "Flying Fortress" and the looks of it.

The B-17, the Flying Fortress, is the best-known heavy bomber of World War II. It was sleek, heavily armored, and had a great name. But it was not the only heavy bomber and not necessarily the best American heavy bomber in the war. There were nearly 13,000 B-17s produced for World War II, but over 18,000 B-24s were produced. The B-24 was not as sleek and was sometimes referred to as "the box the B-17 came in". It was definitely the ugly duckling of the American heavy bombers, but it was effective. When fully loaded, the B-24 could not fly as high as the B-17, reaching a maximum effective height of 23,000 feet compared to 27,000 for the B-17. But the B-24 could carry a significantly larger payload. While both could theoretically carry 8,000 pounds of bombs, the B-17 often had a 3,000-pound load for long range missions, while the B-24 usually had about 5,000 pounds of bombs for the longer missions. Also, the B-24 could fly faster, but in the European Theater of Operations (ETO), since many of the missions used both B-17s and B-24s, this speed advantage was somewhat negated. The wings being mounted lower on the B-17 made emergency landings a little safer, while the high wing mount on the B-24 was more challenging in emergency situations.

The Liberator was also not as safe against anti-aircraft fire. This was an issue in the European Theater of Operation because so much flying was done over enemy occupied territory. The Allied forces might face flak not only over the target, but possibly on much of the route to and from the target. While in the Pacific Theater of Operation (PTO), where most of the flying was over the ocean and very little over enemy occupied territory, the B-24 with its faster speed was the better bomber.

Ken's first flight in a B-24 was on May 17, but there is no letter that survived to provide his description of the experience.

Ken received a card from Marge with several mentions of Katy.

Card from Marjorie 1943:

I received a lovely letter from Katy yesterday and also a swell snapshot of her. It really was a good one too.

Saw your letter in the H + H. Katy also saw it. She speaks well of you, … Muriel is coming down tonight. She still thinks the world of you.

It is interesting that Katy sent Marge a picture, one thing that is absent from Ken's military items is a picture of this girl who captured his heart during the war.

The other interesting item from the note in this card is the reference to the H+H (*Herald of Holiness*). The letter Ken had written which was published is in Figure 36 and in it Ken shares how he heard that a soldier attended a church and was not as welcomed as he thought he should have been. So, Ken shared about his very positive experience at the St. Louis church while he was stationed at Scott Field in Illinois. The letter was published and several friends and family members indicated that they saw the letter when they wrote to Ken. In this case, his sister Marge mentioned that Katy knew about this and must have mentioned it in her letter. This would not be surprising, since the church Ken was promoting was the church at which he met Katy.

The support of the soldiers in training by the local churches during the war was amazing. To think that these churches, which were sometimes very small, would welcome soldiers into their church and then bring them into their homes, feeding them and supporting them was indicative of what churches could be.

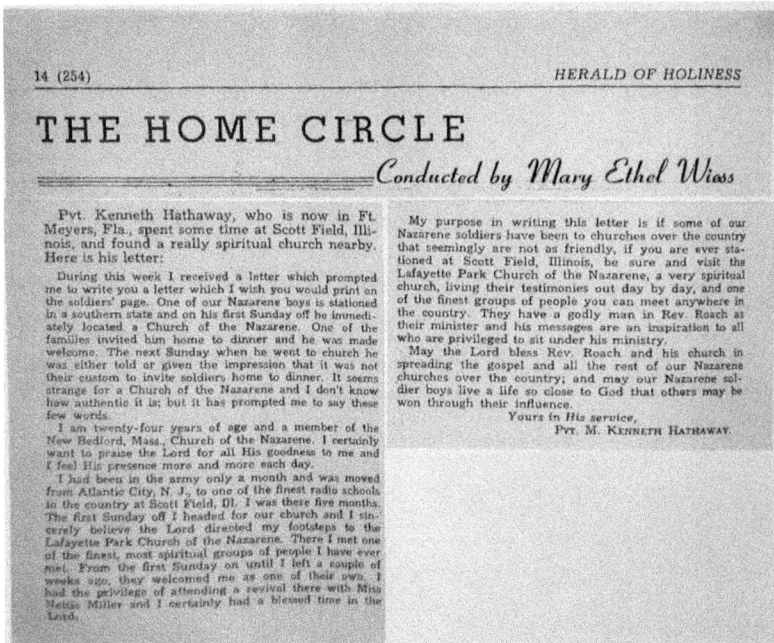

Figure 36. Ken's letter published in the Herald of Holiness.

Ken continued to try and answer his brother's questions, in this case about promotions. Ken also indicated that he was the 1st radio operator on the squadron command plane. With the crew about to head to another training location, this meant that there would be some higher-ranking officers joining them on their plane for the trip.

June 1, 1943:

On your questions I understand that only a certain percent of those graduating from Flying Cadet School make 2nd Lieutenant the next flight officer. It is around the top 10% or 20% something like that. I don't know why they don't become 2nd Lieutenant; it is just a new ruling the army put through. You have no choice in what you pilot and as far as the furlough I understand we will probably get one on completion of our 3rd phase prior to going across. By now you have read my letter in connection with being 1st Radio Operator on the Squadron Command plane. Seeing I have been lucky enough to get this job I am not going to bother applying for flying cadet. In a V formation my plane is first plane. I certainly got a swell break here and it will be fun flying down to Florida and around the islands.

It has rained all day today making three rainy days in a row. Hope it isn't stormy tomorrow. I have a Colonel, Captain, and Lieutenant going down in my plane.

The transition from Boise, ID to Orlando, FL took from June 2 to June 10. This was due to a number of issues which are outlined below.

June 2, 1943:

Left Boise at 9:00 A.M. It was rough all the way down. Landed in El Paso, Texas at 2:30 P.M. The Lieutenant Colonel grounded the plane because we had a leaky gas tank.

June 3, 1943:

Pilot, co-pilot and two engineers tested the plane but it leaked even worse.

Figure 37. June 3, 1943, postcard with a B-25, Fort Bliss Texas, El Paso.

Here is a B-25 (Figure 37). We stopped here yesterday afternoon and stayed all night. Had a leaky gasoline tank. Made it here in 5 ½ hours. Went to prayer meeting last night and stayed all night at the minister's house.

June 9, 1943:

Left El Paso and ran into a storm so we tried to get above it. We put on our oxygen masks and got up to 23,000 feet when the governor on our propeller let go and we had to stop our engine. As the storm was up around 35,000 feet and we had a dead engine we came down and started looking for a field. We decided to land in Jackson Mississippi. We got the propeller fixed in about two hours but the Captain decided to stay overnight.

June 10, 1943:

Left Jackson at 10:00 A.M. and arrived at Tallahassee Florida at 12:15 P.M. Upon landing we discovered that the gas tank was leaking but continued on just the same. We got something to eat and were about through when we had one of the worse electrical storms I've seen. You couldn't see 20 feet ahead. Just before the storm two P-49s cracked up. The storm finally let up and we took off leaving our bomb bay doors open because of the leaking gas. We ran into part of the storm but finally arrived at Orlando at 7:00 P.M.

As part of Ken's continued training, there were numerous demonstrations of various weapons.

June 11. 1943:

In the morning we had lectures on our intelligence department, gasses, airplane recognition. In the afternoon we went to a demonstration of all the Air Corps weapons. They fired all the guns and threw hand grenades. The final thing was the 300 lb. bomb. Dirt flew into the air for 100 feet. It caused a 30 ft. hole.

Orlando, Florida

The reason for the Orlando, FL assignment was not immediately clear because it was so short. Ken was there less than a month and evidently so busy that he did not write much during that time. Other than additional time flying, there was little explanation as to the purpose of this location assignment.

June 25, 1943:

We have been very busy with no time to write. Yesterday we flew for 8 ½ hrs. I will write more about what happened etc. later.

We were allowed to come into town tonight after being restricted a whole week. Rather than catch up on letter writing I thought I would come in town as it is change from camp. I wanted to get a good meal too as yesterday we didn't have anything to eat from 11:30 AM to midnight.

Will also try and get a letter off to Muriel tomorrow or Sunday.

June 26, 1943:

Before I forget don't write anymore letters here as I am leaving Wed. I believe for Wendover Field, Utah.

I haven't been doing a lot of radio operating when flying around here but we do the following:

Ken included a fair amount of coding in the letter which is pictured in Figure 38.

At this point Ken was assigned to the 714th squadron of the 448 Bomb Group.

June 26, 1943:

I should get Tech Sergeant on this model crew as I am 1st Radio operator. I can't make any kind of officer unless I went to officer's School. After my 2nd and 3rd phase we are subject to overseas duty. I am in the 448 Bomb Group and our Squadron is one of four in the group, the 714th. When our bomb group goes over we all go. I believe I will get a furlough before going over sometime in Sept.

Figure 38. Letter with some sample codes on the lower half.

Our second armorer tends to the tail gun, armorer left waist gun, asst engineer right waist gun, engineer upper turret, bombardier nose guns, asst radio operator has the hatch gun. It is a hole in the floor a little behind the waist guns. When we go across we have a belly turret on the plane and also a turret in the nose instead of the hand held guns. I don't handle a gun unless someone is killed or wounded as far as I know now.

Thursday – We took off at 3:00 PM with 6 ships in two V formations. We headed out over the Gulf and as we neared our bombing target mobile, we had dropped our bombs in the ocean, we were attacked by 20 P-47's. They swarmed all over us. By this time we had about 12 B-24's and some B-17s. The sky was full of planes. They made behind attacks on us for about an hour. Just before we got to Mobile we ran into a storm and got separated for a while from our squadron. We didn't get back until 11:30 PM and got to bed around 1:00 AM. We borrowed another plane as ours wasn't ready. We were up around 25,000 feet using oxygen.

Friday – Didn't do too much all day. Worked around the plane. Went into town at night and went to an N.Y.P.S. social. Had a swell time staying until 10:30 P.M. I got back to camp and four of the six of us in my tent were drunk. We didn't get to sleep until 1:00 A.M. they made so much noise and the engineer who didn't go to town told us we have to get up at 3:00 AM to fly, so all we had was two hours sleep and I am tired. The engineer and myself moved today to another tent so we could get some sleep nights.

We had a briefing at 4:30 AM. This consists of telling us where we are going, the weather, what opposition we will meet etc. It was pouring out. We went to the plane and checked everything and was taxiing out when the ground station called back each ship and told them due to bad weather all flights were called off.

June 27, 1943:

Morning flight called off. While waiting for a ride into town my Co-Pilot came up and told me to change immediately as we had an Alert Mission. We flew for an hour but it was pretty rough and two others and myself got sick.

June 28, 2943:

Took off at 9:30 A.M. heading for Baton Rouge, Louisiana. There were 6 of us in formation and as we neared Mobile Alabama at 19,000 feet when one of our engines started to act funny. We left the formation and came back to the field fighting rough and stormy weather.

Chapter 6

Training: Utah/Iowa

The next training stop was to be Wendover Aerial Gunnery School in Utah where there was more gunnery and flying practice. The base was fairly isolated and would have been very hot in the summer.

The following is a quote from another flier who was stationed at Wendover during the War.

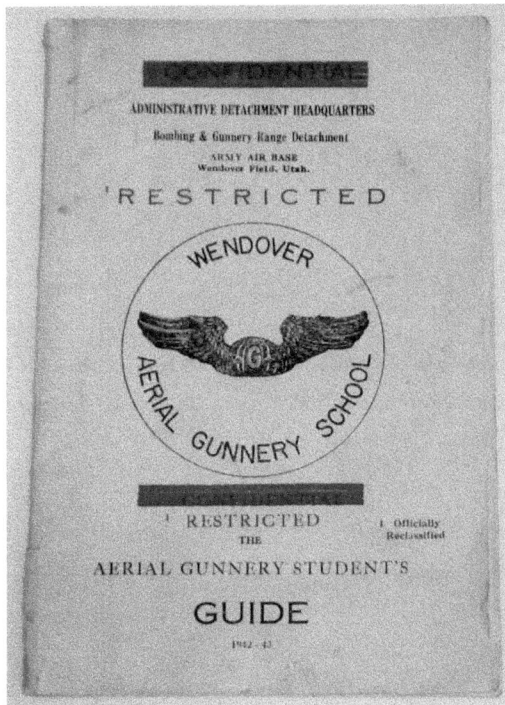

Figure 39. Wendover Aerial Gunnery School Guide.

Wendover Aerial Gunnery School, Utah, was way up in the hills. It was so remote that the GI comment was, a man going AWOL for five days would only be charged for three because he could be seen walking on the salt flats for the first two days. If ever a place could be classified as a sample of hell this was the place. June and July, with temperature near 100 degrees F (38 degrees C), was unbearable. It was so hot that I had to cool off with a shower whenever possible, usually several times a day, and this was not easy because we had to rely on water trucked in from the air base on a 24-hour basis. Wendover was the only gunnery school without flying training. (Bowman, M. W. (2010). *The Mighty Eighth at War: USAAF 8th AirForce Bombers Versus the Luftwaffe 1943-1945*. Pen and Sword Aviation, p. 64).

Figure 40. Birthday card to Ken from his mom that contained a censored letter inside.

The last line in the above quote is interesting because maybe there wasn't official flight training at Wendover as claimed in this quote, but there were clearly practice flights.

Ken left Florida on June 30, 1943, stopped in Chicago and Sioux City, IA and arrived at Wendover Field, UT July 4, 1943.

It was a long time before Ken received a furlough, but that might have been because his training took longer than some other soldiers. This could have been because of his foot injury back in New Jersey, and the position he was training for, which probably required more training than some other positions. Whatever the reason, some of those from back home noticed how long it was before his first furlough.

Card from Dud, July 1943:

Well, it is almost a year since you left to start your Army career but to me it seems 4 or 5 years. I am trusting and praying that I will see you soon and that before another year is over this terrible war will end.

Card from Mrs. Costa July 1943:

Received your card and letter and was so glad to hear from you. However as welcome as your letters have been, we miss you and wish we could see you. Seems that all the other boys who went around the same time or after you did have dropped around to see us sometime or other. Don't you think it's about time you paid us a visit.

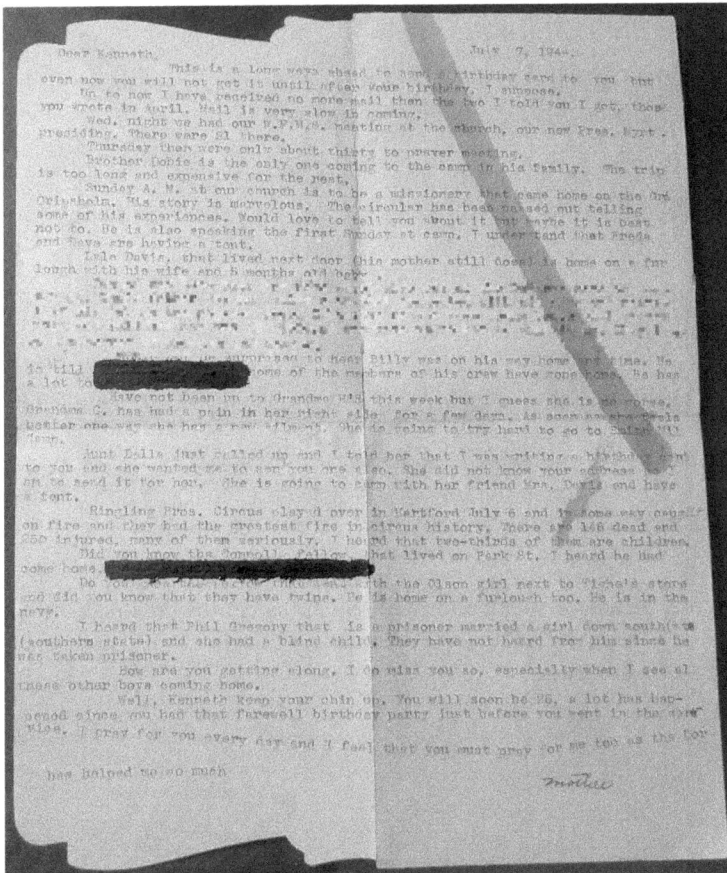

Figure 41. The censored letter from the birthday card in figure 40. One paragraph has been blurred because it contained sensitive personal information.

The censors were always working to ensure confidential material was not being shared. The letter in Figure 41 is the inside of the card in Figure 40 and shows some of the censor's handiwork. Ken's mother also made a small age mistake in this letter since Ken was going to turn 25 in early August not 26.

July 7, 1943, early censored birthday card from Ken's mom:

I would not be surprised to hear Billy was on his way home any time. He is still ▮▮▮▮▮▮ some of the members of his crew have gone home. He has a lot to ▮▮▮▮▮▮

"Did you know the Connolly fellow, that lived on Park St. I heard he had come home. ▮▮▮▮▮"

Well. Kenneth keep your chin up. You will soon be 26, a lot has happened since you had that farewell birthday party just before you went in the service. I pray for you every day and I feel that you must pray for me as the Lord has helped me so much.

Ken continued to have shooting practice, since in combat he might have to man a gun if another crew member was injured.

July 10, 1943:

Qualified for marksmanship on the rifle range scoring 72 out of possible 100 points.

There were constant mishaps and issues that happened during flights.

July 16, 1943:

Flew from 8:00 A.M. to 9:00 A.M. While flying our gas cap came loose and gas began to spill all over the place. The pilot immediately shut that engine off and radioed the field for an emergency landing. We landed with only two engines going. Both the engines that were out were on the same side. The ground crew fixed the gas cap and we flew again from 10:00 A.M. until noon.

It is pretty amazing that the pilot was able to safely land the plane with both engines out on one side. It also was amazing that they went up again in the same plane an hour later!

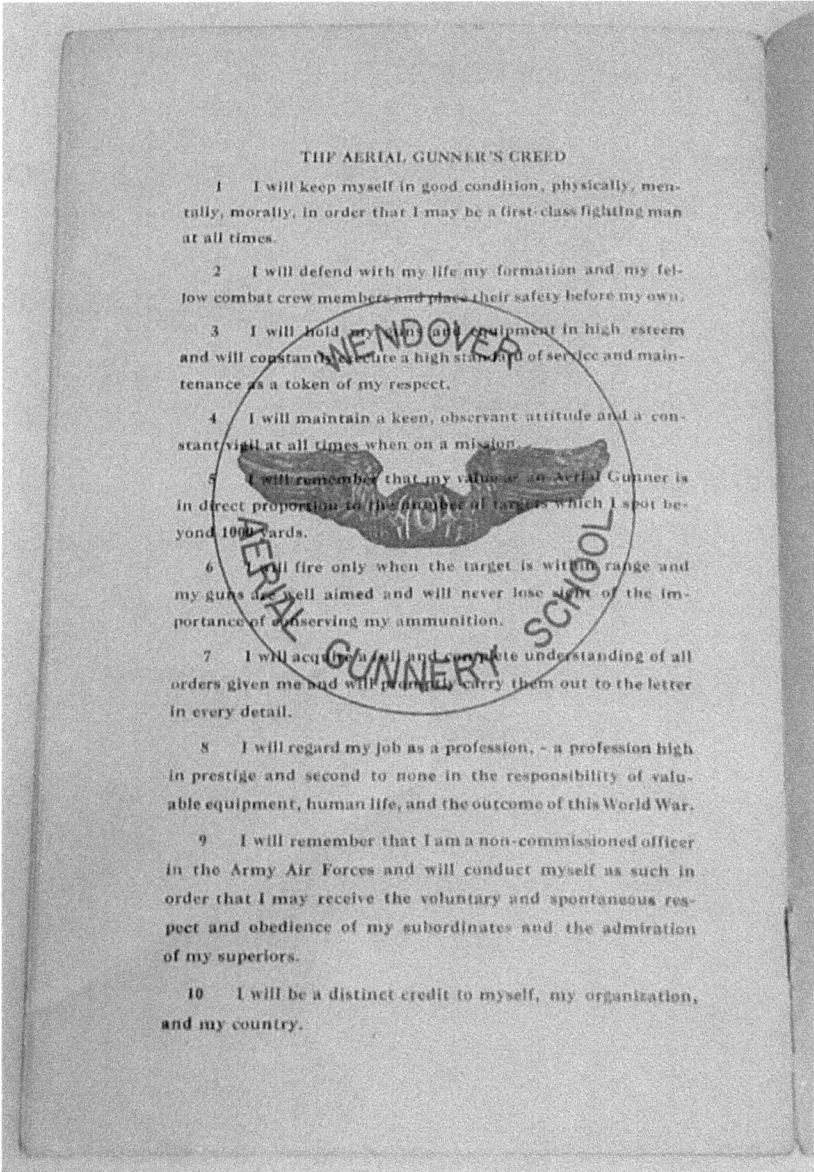

Figure 42. Aerial Gunners Creed, from the guide in Figure 39.

As the time was getting closer to Ken actually going overseas, the seriousness of what he was facing was sinking in. In his scrapbook is a Last Will and Testament dated July 28, 1943, leaving everything to his mother, who he also named as his executrix. While an executrix was typically female, nowadays no matter the sex, the person charged to carry out the terms of a will is called the executor. Through it all Ken kept the faith.

July 30, 1943:

I have been realizing how dangerous my job is especially since we are sure to go across soon. I know I am where I should be spiritually but lately I have been doing a lot of thinking about it. Pray for me that somehow I will get a bigger vision on the spiritual life and give my all to Christ. I still keep away from all worldly things and would rather go to church than anything else.

If you don't hear from me for a few days it is because I am so busy. From now on we will be getting busier and busier. They are certainly getting us ready for combat.

The crews were still being adjusted with positions switching, and new crew members replacing old members.

July 30, 1943:

They have broken up our crew. My co-pilot is now my pilot and we have a new co-pilot who used to be a pilot of a P-40. We also have a new navigator and bombardier. All the enlisted men are the same with me as first radio operator. We haven't any asst. engineer as yet.

Figure 43. Another card Ken received.

Ken was still hoping that things would work out with Katy, though her closing a letter with "to a wonderful friend" was probably not the endearment he was hoping for.

August 6, 1943:

I also received a swell box of candy made by the Famous-Barr company of St. Louis from Katy and Betty together. Betty is a very nice looking brunette. I was up to her house a couple of times to eat. All in all I did very well on my Birthday. Katy also sent me a swell birthday card today in which it said to a wonderful friend.

The weather affected training and war for the Air Corps probably more than almost all the other branches of the military. Despite the best preparations, bad weather would occasionally spring up and impact the training, but it served as good practice for combat.

August 6, 1943:

This morning I went out to the skeet range but didn't fire a shot. There was one box of shells short so I happened to be the unlucky one and not shoot. I told the lieutenant about it when I got back and he was a little sore about it and wanted to know why they didn't take enough. This afternoon I went to school and I was to fly tonight from 5:45 PM until 11:30 P.M. We took off at 5:45 P.M. and had flown a little over an hour when we ran into a swell thunderstorm. Boy, did it rain. It just came down in torrents. We flew for a while in it and then landed to pick up another lieutenant to do some work on the bombsight. We had no more taken off again when it began to get worse and worse. Finally the pilot decided it was getting too bad and called it quits. Boy was it rough up there. The ship was rocking all over the sky. We landed about a half hour ago and I thought I would write a couple of letters before retiring for the night. It is thundering real bad right now and pouring outside which is unusual for Wendover. I was having a swell time working the radio and the ground station was coming in so clear I hated to come down. I sent in two position reports and received one weather report, also had to tune up our command set, which is the pilot's set, while in flight. I closed down my radio and went to the rear of the ship up on top of the bomb bay and tuned his set up. I sure like radio it is very interesting and a lot of fun.

Ken described the crash of a B-24 from the 399th Bomb Group August 9, 1943:

A B-24 of the 399th Bomb Group crashed on railroad tracks causing 26 railroad cars to go off the track. The co-pilot was killed, the bombardier and two others of the crew were not expected to live.

Bomber Crash Landing Wrecks Freight Train

WENOVER, Utah, Aug. 9 (AP)
—An Army bomber crash landed on the Western Pacific tracks near here last night and 10 minutes later a freight train was wrecked as it plowed into parts of the bomber.

Second Lieutenant Richard L. Blue of Rantoul, Ill., was injured fatally in the bomber crash. Ten other flyers were hurt, some critically.

None of the trainmen, who aided the flyers from their battered bomber, was hurt.

Figure 44. Newspaper article on bomber crash of August 9, 1943.

While there were training accidents in all types of warplanes, the B-24, occasionally called the "flying coffin", may have been more prone to accidents than the B-17. The B-24 was quickly developed primarily during war time, when quantity was important, while the B-17 was designed and produced before the war started. The Liberators did not have self-sealing equipment like the Flying Fortress; leaks were more common, which led to the B-24 being more prone to catch fire. In 1943 alone, there were 298 B-24 accidents that took the lives of 850 crewmen and probably injured many more. The "Flying Boxcar" was an effective aircraft but it did have its own challenges.

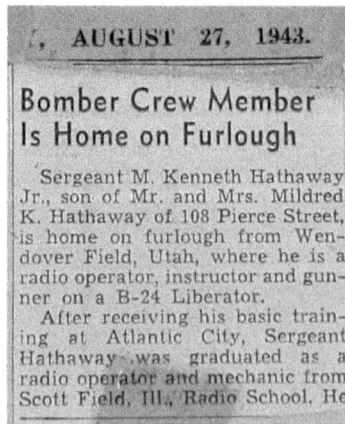

AUGUST 27, 1943.

Bomber Crew Member Is Home on Furlough

Sergeant M. Kenneth Hathaway Jr., son of Mr. and Mrs. Mildred K. Hathaway of 108 Pierce Street, is home on furlough from Wendover Field, Utah, where he is a radio operator, instructor and gunner on a B-24 Liberator.

After receiving his basic training at Atlantic City, Sergeant Hathaway was graduated as a radio operator and mechanic from Scott Field, Ill., Radio School. He

Figure 45. Newspaper article on Ken's furlough.

Furlough finally arrived. Ken came home to New Bedford, MA on August 24, 1943 (over a year after he left for Fort Devens) and returned to Utah on

August 31, 1943. This was certainly a sign that the training was nearing an end and he would be sent overseas before much longer.

Card September 1943 Mrs. Costa:

It was so nice to have you here at home with us and to know that you enjoyed your furlough.

Ken did a lot of flying while at Wendover. On September 6, he said that they had done 50 hours of flying over the last 5 days, sometimes on short rations.

September 6, 1943:

Well here I am up around 10,000 feet. We are going up all the time and will be at 14,000 ft soon. We haven't oxygen masks so that is as high as we will go. I didn't expect to fly tonight but we have just taken off. It is 7:30 P.M. I also have a flight tomorrow night. It has been two hours since I started this letter and what trouble, there is so much static in the air I haven't been able to contact the ground station. My tracking wire antenna got stuck and I had to pull 50 ft of it in by hand. We will probably land soon.

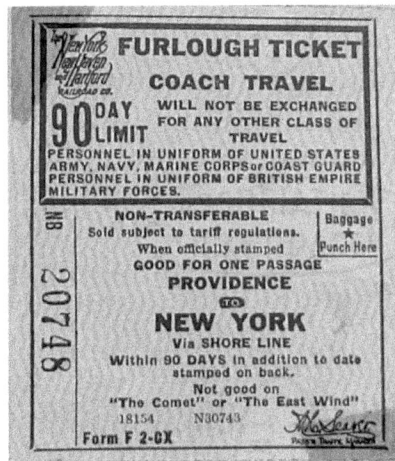

Figure 46. Furlough ticket.

Well here it is another day and I am in the plane again waiting to go up. It is 9:00 A.M. and we will fly until 12:30 P.M. We didn't get in until almost midnight last night with the radio. I finally got the ground station as we were landing.

Yesterday morning I went to school for a couple of hours and in the afternoon went out to the range and shot the 45 caliber pistol. I did fair in it. I also shot the 30 cal. Carbine which is like a rifle. I did very good in that getting two bullseyes and making 38 points out of a possible 50. I then flew last night as I mentioned before, we may fly again tonight too. I am certainly getting plenty of flying in anyway.

I am back in the plane again taxiing out on the runway. This afternoon my crew went out to the skeet range and shot skeet; I didn't do so good. I only got 10 out of 25. When we came back to the operations office at 5:00 P.M. they informed us we had to report back at 6:00 P.M. to fly. I had watermelon and two slices of bread and peanut butter for supper. Had hardly any dinner at all. We each have a quart of milk in the plane as we are pretty hungry. My pilot ate his first meal today in two and a half days. It is now 6:45 P.M. and we will fly until around 10:30 P.M. I have to get up at 6:00 A.M. tomorrow morning and fly again 7:30 A.M. to 12:30 A.M. in formation. That will make 50 hours of flying in 5 days. Boy are they working us hard.

Ken received word that they would be moving to the next stage of their training in Sioux City, IA. He wrote this note as their plane was taking off for a training run.

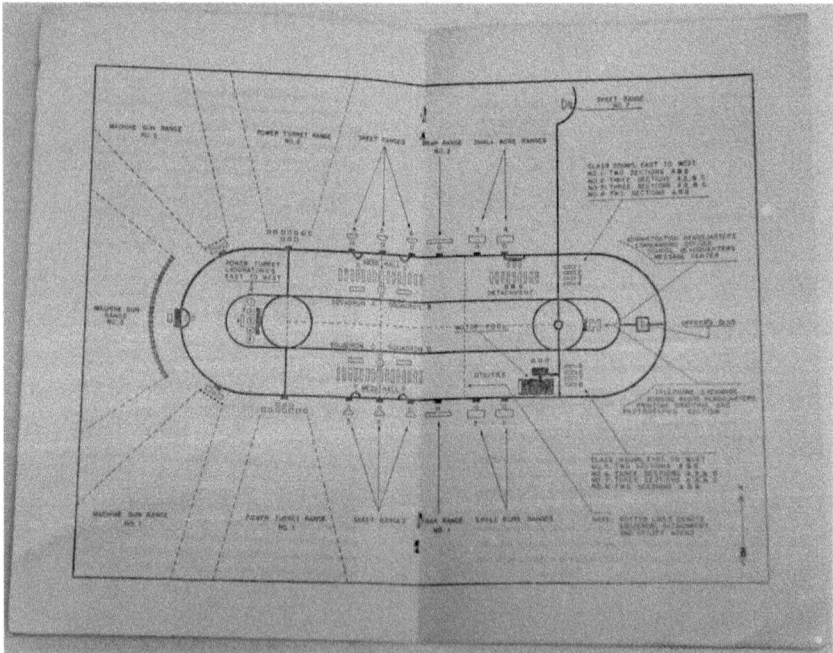

Figure 47. Layout of the base at Wendover, taken from the guide in Figure 39.

September 6, 1943:

Well I finally have good news. Don't write any more letters to here as we are leaving next Tuesday for Sioux City, Iowa. The Nebraska deal fell through. I would rather go to Sioux City anyway. We are now ready to take off and I am turning my radio on. Here we go, 40, 60, 80, 100, and 110 mph and we are now taking off. We are climbing about 500 feet a minute. Now it is 1000ft. Will continue writing as soon as I call in to the ground station. … I have been a half hour trying to get the ground station to answer me. What a job. I finally got them and they said my signal strength and readability was good. We are now at 12,000 ft. over the bombing range. The bomb bay doors are open and we will be dropping our bombs soon.

Ken was still trying to win Katy over. With a new navigator who happened to be from St. Louis, Ken was hopeful that he might get a chance to see her, but there is no evidence that his hope became a reality.

September 6, 1943:

I am sure anxious to get to St. Louis. Our navigator's wife lives three blocks from Katy and he says we will have to get to St. Louis some way or another. I sure hope so.

More training accidents.

September 6, 1943:

I suppose you read about the two crack ups we had here. One, I believe a week ago yesterday and one yesterday. All were killed. I believe 19 in the two crashes. It wasn't our group but the 399th Bomb Group. They have had tough luck lately with their planes. The opinion is that both were the pilots fault. I am glad we have a good pilot and a good engineer that watches out for anything that might go wrong.

September 11, 1943:

On that B-17 crash the pilot was dead when he pulled him out and the co-pilot was bad off. He died later at the hospital.

As a natural part of flying, equipment would sometimes break down. The more practice flights, the more opportunities for these unexpected incidents that would also serve as preparation for things that might go wrong during combat.

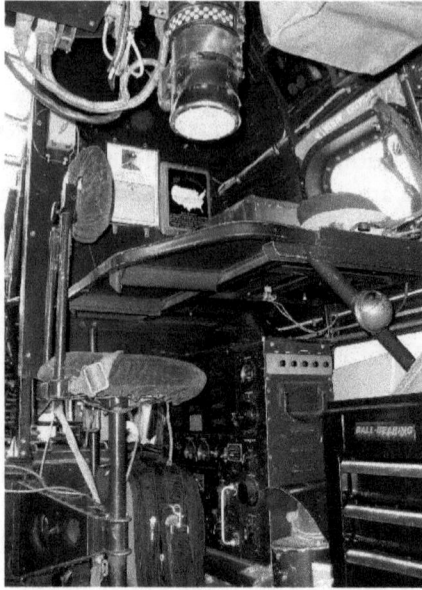

Figure 48. Radio compartment on a B-24 Liberator.

September 6, 1943:

I just fixed the interphone in the upper turret for the navigator so he can listen in on the radio. He is a swell fellow.

September 11, 1943:

Well Thursday night we only flew for an hour and a half. Just before we landed a fuse blew in the pilot's radio set. I finally got the thing fixed and we landed at 8:00 P.M.

There were various training flights every day, and in some cases multiple times a day.

September 11, 1943:

Friday morning we flew from 9:00 A.M. to 12:30 P.M. I had a half hour for dinner and went to the cafeteria to eat. I then had to attend a lecture for ¾ of an hour. At 3:00 P.M. I had to go to Panoramic Gunnery for an hour. This is where you shoot at planes flashed on the screen. We were to fly last night but the flight was canceled.

I had to get up at 2:00 A.M. this morning and was to fly from 3:30 A.M. to 8:30 A.M. We took off at 3:30 A.M. and at 4:00 A.M. landed with #4 engine almost out. It was running bad. As they couldn't get it fixed we called the flight off and I got back into bed at 5:00 A.M. I slept until 10:00

A.M. and just had a shower, shaved and went over to see about some mail. I drew a blank this morning although I had expected one from Katy.

September 27, 1943:

Once more I am writing from the air. We are skimming along the ground about 100 ft up going 180 M.P.H. It is 8:30 AM Monday. It is a lot of fun flying like this. We just went over a small town and passed over a school house. You could see the children faces as they looked up we were so low. The pilot is making a turn now and as I look out my window it looks as though our wing would hit the tree tops. I could have sworn we were going to hit those trees we just passed. We are racing an automobile now. Swish, shucks that was no race we are a mile ahead of him in a few seconds.

Thankfully, not all training accidents resulted in the loss of lives. Below, Ken mentions a crash in which, thankfully, no lives were lost. Figure 49 references the crash.

September 13, 1943:

Flew from 7:00 A.M. to 9:00 A.M. in a three plane formation to Elko Nevada and back. From 9:00 A.M. to 12:20 P.M. we had to attend a lecture, pack our stuff, eat and get a medical check for flying. We were in the plane at 12:30 P.M., almost an hour before take off to check off the equipment. At 1:20 P.M. the first of the ten planes took off. The rest of the planes took off at 30 second intervals. We were the last plane. I noticed we were not climbing properly so I looked out of the Pilot's window. About a mile from us on the desert was one of our planes. We could see skid marks on the ground. Some of the fellows   were standing around outside the plane. Two fellows broke their legs. We circled the plane and then continued on, arriving at Sioux City, Iowa at 9:30 P.M.

Wendover Bomber Crashes

WENDOVER FIELD—The full crew of 11 men of an army bomber escaped injuries this morning shortly after 8 p.m. when the plane was forced to make a crash landing and burned in the Salt Flats 15 miles south of the air base.

According to First Lt. A. J. Madden, public relations officer, the plane skidded on its belly for more than a half mile and one of the engines caught fire during the landing. However, all members of the crew were able to get out of the plane with only minor bruises before the bomber was engulfed in flames. It burned for several hours, according to reports.

The plane was on a routine flight at the time of the crash. A board of inquiry has been appointed to investigate the crash, Lieutenant Madden said.

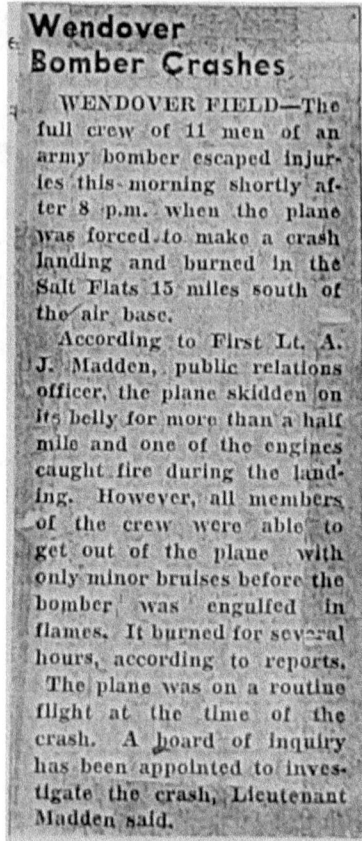

Figure 49. Newspaper article on bomber crash in the desert.

At this stage of the training, part of their work was to practice taking long flights, formation flights, and high altitude flights to simulate the experience that they would have flying from England to occupied Europe.

September 20, 1943:

Flew in the morning. Circled Kansas City at 8:45 A.M. My radio transmitter kept going out. We flew near Omaha Nebraska.

September 26, 1943:

Took off at 2:00 P.M. and flew to St Paul and Minneapolis in formation with another plane and then flew to Watertown. Did some bombing at 20,000 feet and landed at the field at 6:25 P.M.

September 28, 1943:

Flew from 7:00 P.M. to 10:00 P.M. Went to Des Moines Iowa.

October 4, 1943, letter

Flew from 6:45 A.M. to 11:45 A.M. in a ten-plane formation at 20,000 feet.

October 7, 1943:

Flew to St. Louis at night 8:00 P.M. to 1:30 A.M.

Another sign that Ken was one of the better Radio Operators was that he was evidently sending in the position reports as instructed. Whether or not this related to his getting a pass is debatable, but his willingness to forfeit a pass to enable him to attend church was emblematic of his commitment to church attendance.

Figure 50. Radio Operator uniform patch.

September 27, 1943:

I slept until 10:00 A.M. Sunday and was I tired. I was supposed to go to school but slept right through it. At 12:00 noon I was over to Operations waiting to fly again. Lt. Miller came up to me and said 'I haven't seen you for a few days. Have you been getting bawled out too?' It seems as though most of the Radio Operators have been getting bawled out after every flight for some reason or another. Usually it is because they didn't send in position reports every half hour. I haven't had any trouble so far. I'll keep my fingers crossed. While talking with Lt. Miller I asked him how the chances were for a pass so I could go to church. Saturday they had put in a new ruling. We were only allowed a pass every three days instead of every other day and my night was tonight. I told him I would forfeit tonight's pass. He said, 'Seeing you are going to church O.K. and you can have your regular one tomorrow night too. I was the only one of my flight that got out, out of 36 men.

I dashed over to my barracks and changed my clothes, got my pass and headed for the gate. I had only had dinner and was starved but I thought

I will eat after church. It was impossible to make N.Y.P.S. I was lucky and only had to wait 5 minutes for the bus. I got into Sioux City at 7:30 P.M. Once again I was lucky and only had to wait a minute for the street car. I got to church at 7:45 P.M. I was in time to hear the two specials by the song evangelists. Just the specials were worth coming out for. Two sisters play the guitars and sing. The evangelist was very good and we had a very good crowd out. After church the minister invited me over to the house to have some more chicken. I sure didn't refuse as I was starved. I had a swell snack and sat around talking until 11:00 P.M. I met a couple of fellows in the streetcar and we decided to try and hitch hike back to camp while waiting for the bus. We were lucky three girls picked us up and we got back at 11:30 P.M.

Ken did a fair amount of letter writing while flying since there was often a reasonable amount of dead time while the crew was in the air—even though pens often did not work well at higher altitudes.

September 27, 1943:

My radio receiver is out and so I have the whole five hours to myself and am catching up on writing. I can't receive a thing. My pilot is sending in the position report over his radio so we are only 5 or 6 miles from the field and he can reach them.

I forgot we were flying so low. I can use a pen if we are below 5,000 ft.

At this point, much of what Ken and the crew did was train for bombing runs. These flights would go higher, be much colder, and would require the crew to wear their oxygen masks.

October 7, 943:

I will give you the news since Monday. I flew Monday night from 8:00 P.M. to 1:30 A.M. We went up to 24,200 ft and was it cold. I had all my fur lined clothes on and was still chilly. My hands began to get so cold I could hardly write at all. My co-pilot froze his feet a little. It was around 10 below zero in the front of the plane with the heater on and 20 below in the back of the ship. I am glad my job keeps me up front.

Tuesday morning I slept until 9:30 A.M. We were supposed to fly from 11:30 A.M. to 5:00 P.M. but the plane wasn't ready so we hung around until 1:30 P.M. before taking off and flew until 7:00 P.M. We flew at 20,000 ft and became the first crew to drop 20 bombs since arriving at this field. We had our oxygen masks on for four hours. It wasn't as cold as the night before.

Again, Ken gave up a longer pass to get a shorter pass so he could attend some church services

October 7, 1943:

Wed morning I was up at 6:00 A.M. We were supposed to fly from 8:00 A.M. to 1:30 P.M. but after hanging around until 11:00 A.M. our flight was finally canceled. I went to school in the afternoon for two hours. I was told at 4:00 P.M. we could get a 16 hr pass. I went over to operations and got an 8 hour pass as I owed them for letting me out last Sunday. We had a large crowd and the evangelist was very good. After church I went over to the minister's house for a couple of hours. I got back to the field at midnight.

It would not be the army without rumors, especially since so little information was given to the typical soldier about future plans. In these cases, as is human nature, the soldiers themselves "thought up" numerous options.

October 7, 1943:

Well rumors are flying thick and thin. Some are we will be broken up as a group as we are not fit for combat, another one we will be a training outfit and stay here, another one we will do costal patrol work. We will know definitely about the situation in three weeks anyways.

Figure 51. Army Air Force technical badge.

Prayers continued to come in as the inevitable transition from training to combat approached

Card October 1943, Mrs. Costa:

Glad to hear the good reports about your work and exams. It's great to get such good marks but don't be too smart or - - - (you know what I mean.)

I want you to know that we who are left behind are praying for you and your quick return to us. According to the reports we get in the paper and radio, we are greatly encouraged and have faith in Him that all will soon be over and we'll have all our beloved boys back with us again.

In mid-Fall 1943, Ken wrote a long passage addressing a variety of issues from grounding himself to a brand-new B-24H plane and its issues.

October 13, 1943:

Sunday night I got a pass for 7 hrs. by forfeiting my 18 hr. pass last night. We had a wonderful closing service and a fine crowd out. After church I went over to the pastor's house and had a swell treat. We talked until 11:15 P.M. and I said "Goodbye" to the evangelist. I then walked home with two girls who were song evangelists. I stood talking with them for a while and got their address so I could drop them a line once in a while if I ever have time. I got back to the field at 12:30 A.M. At 1:00 A.M. I was in my flying clothes and at Operations ready to fly. We flew from 2:00 A.M. to 7:00 A.M. Was I tired. I couldn't keep my eyes open hardly. I got to bed at 8:00 A.M. Monday morning. I could only sleep three hours as we were to fly again that afternoon. I was up at 11:00 A.M. ate and at 1:00 P.M. was over to Operations. My crew flew but for the first time since I have been flying I had to ground myself. I felt rotten. I had a headache; my stomach was on the rocks and in general I wasn't fit to fly at high altitude for 5 hours. I hung around in the afternoon and rested and went to bed at 10:00 P.M. Once again I didn't get much sleep as I had to get up at 3:30 A.M. to fly again. We were supposed to take off at 5:30 A.M. but we had a brand new B-24H assigned to us and we had to wait until they put guns in the plane and oxygen. We were already to taxi out on the runway when the pilot's radio wouldn't work. I tried to fix it but finally had to give up. The ground mechanic came up and we had to have a new dynamotor put in. We finally took off around 8:00 A.M. We flew at 20,000 ft. The weather was bad and closing in fast. At 11:00 A.M. we decided to come down and find the field. We came down to 8,000 ft and there was a solid blanket of clouds below us. We tried to find an open spot to go through but couldn't. We flew around and finally 30 miles from the field we were able to barely see the ground. We came down to 5,000 ft and headed toward the field with the clouds just above us. Finally we had to get down to 2,500 ft. We were 10 miles from the field when the tower called us and told us to land right away as the weather was closing in fast. All ships were called in. We landed at 11:40 A.M. and 20 minutes after landing we had a downpour. It rained all afternoon and part of the evening and thundered and lightened. I went to Radio school and when I got back to the barracks I found we were to have a smack down inspection of all equipment.

The issue of new clothing and equipment was another sign that the transition to overseas combat was fast approaching.

October 13, 1943:

All equipment that isn't good for six months or is worn is to be replaced. I am getting two new pair of shoes, new overcoat, field jacket, summer flying suit, goggles, stockings etc. I think we will be leaving here in a couple of weeks.

Another famous American celebrity/athlete Ken was able to see while in the military was Joe Louis in a boxing match. (Joseph Louis Barrow (1914-1981), known as "the Brown Bomber" was the world heavyweight champion for 11 years, from 1937 to 1949, setting an all-time record for that title. He successfully defended his title 25 times after earning it June 22, 1937, at only age 23; 21 of those title bouts were between December 1940 and June 1941. Of special interest in the WWII era, Louis lost to German heavyweight Max Schmelling in 1936, but re-gained the title with a first round KO in 1938. Schmelling was highly favored by the Nazis, but was not a Nazi, himself, but their 1938 rematch was portrayed as "Nazism v. Democracy." During WWII, Louis entered the Army in 1942, serving in an all-Black unit with legendary baseball player Jackie Robinson. Louis fought 96 short exhibition bouts while touring over 2 million troops. He donated $100,000 to the war effort, as well. For more information, see: https://www.britannica.com/biography/Joe-Louis).

October 13, 1943:

Well last night I'll bet you can't guess who I saw, No it wasn't Katy. I saw Joe Louis in action. He boxed three two minute rounds. We had four bouts altogether. It lasted an hour and was good.

Ken continued to show serious interest in Katy along with very conservative views, even for Nazarenes. He did not seem to have an issue with a girl sitting on his lap!

October 13, 1943:

It looks like our Nazarenes are slipping. I shouldn't think a minister's wife should go bowling. I know one thing Katy is a real Nazarene. She (I am answering part of Marge's letter now) told me once if I married a St. Louis girl I wouldn't be able to give her a diamond. I don't know whether she was hinting at herself or not. I hope so

Too bad N.Y.P.S. isn't going as good as it should. There was sure an opportunity there. Katy wants me to come to St. Louis and be President of their society. I told her I would if she would be Secretary and sit on my knee. She said it was all right with her. However, I think I have had enough of being Pres. of an N.Y.P.S.

On the other hand, the girl who was a friend from the church back home and had hopes for a deeper relationship with Ken was evidently reading the writing on the wall.

October 13, 1943:

I still would like to know when I wrote that letter to Freda. I have just looked over last two letters to me and as no mention was made of Muriel in her letters. I know I didn't mention anything. The last letter I wrote her was dated July sometimes and I hadn't written since May or June before then. It makes me feel bad to think she is spreading things around. As for mentioning Katy I might have said I met a swell girl in St. Louis or something like that but I have said that about other places too but haven't hinted of anything being serious.

Ken was still answering Dud's questions about things related to the plane and the military.

October 13, 1943:

About the lighting system in the plane. Well I have a light above my desk but during flight I can't use it as it blinds the pilot. I take off the cover to my receiver and use the lights there that light up the dials. It covers the whole desk and you can see pretty good. There is one in the bomb bay and a couple in the rear of the ship. Also there is one up over the bomb bay where some of the radio equipment is.

I converse with the Navigator mostly on my flights asking him for our position etc. Sometimes I talk with the pilot if I am having radio trouble.

November 3, 1943:

Everyone can hear everyone else talk over the interphone.

We put our brakes on only on the ground. In order to slow up in the air you have to pull your throttles back.

Little issues continued to plague some of their flights.

October 20, 1943:

We were supposed to fly in a 10-plane formation to Texas, Colorado, Arkansas, Oklahoma and back. We left at 12:05 P.M. but our landing gear kept falling down so we landed. In the afternoon we went on a bombing mission to Minnesota.

November 1, 1943:

Flew in a 19-plane formation. Developed engine trouble (supercharger on #1 engine let go) so had to come back to the field.

The time to finally go overseas was quickly approaching.

October 24, 1943:

Flew from 11 A.M. until 2 P.M. in a 15-plane formation at 20,000 feet. We were restricted until after our "Preparatory to Overseas Movement Inspection."

In the next letter, Ken talks about the members of his crew, these were the ones that he would fly with once they got over to England. The crew had their official picture taken and had sent some copies home.

November 3, 1943:

Lt Miller is no longer my pilot. He is the Operations Officer now. He has charge of scheduling our flights. We received our crew picture today alongside 010.

Figure 52. The crew picture. Top row (left to right), Hennessy, Walker, Carroll, Smith, Middle Row, Brown, Childs, Laing, Hathaway. Front row Schiefelbein, Miltner.

My pilot is Lt. Carroll, a swell fellow and one of the best pilots in the squadron.

My Co-pilot is Lt. Walker who we just got a couple of weeks ago.

Lt. Smith from St. Louis is the navigator and another swell fellow. One of the best navigators around.

Lt. Hennessy is the Bombardier a rebel from Georgia. He is another swell fellow and a whale of a bombardier.

Earl Brown is the engineer and a good one. We chum together around camp.

Childs is asst engineer and a very good gunner. We just got him last week. We got rid of our other Asst engineer.

Miltner is our armored gunner and a good shot.

Schefelbein is our tail gunner and a whale of a shot. He was an Instructor at Wendover Aerial Gunnery School for 10 months.

Laing is my asst and the lower ball gunner.

We really have a swell crew all told and ought to do plenty of damage over there.

Ken's romance with Katy was starting to heat up, thanks in part to a long phone conversation he was able to have with her. The timing of this is interesting, since Ken was not too far away from going overseas at this point. Earlier, he had mentioned not wanting to get serious with Muriel because of going overseas to combat, but evidently when it came to Katy he had a different perspective.

Card from Katy, November 5, 1943:

Finally got some of the wedding pictures. They are not much good, but at least you can tell who we are! And that's not saying much!

How do you feel after that telephone call? I hope you are still okay! I am still sorta worried about all that money you spend though. If you keep on you'll find out how awful a catch I am. Ha.

Card from Katy November 8, 1943:

Well, I am wondering where you are right now. Probably you have left camp already. I had the blues all day today and I didn't sleep a wink last night. I stayed with Betty the "rest" of the night. My old heart sure feels heavy every time I think about you leaving! I was just about to give you up last night on that call. Another 5 minutes and I would have been in the bed. Love & lots of it Katy.

Christmas 1943 card from Aunt Annie:

…your mother received your letter today. The letter I refer to is the one where you talked with Katy for one hour. I take it that it was successful and promising.

Another note from the always faithful Mrs. Costa.

Promotion card from Mrs. Costa dated November 7, 1943:

Was so glad to hear from you again and to hear of your most recent promotion. Wish you the very best of luck in your new job and your new venture, I pray that the Lord will be with you, give you strength and courage always no matter where you may be. I know you will keep true and He will not fail you.

One "assignment" that was really surprising was when Ken ended up on the chain gang, an assignment for those soldiers who had committed a serious infraction, but there was no indication what the accusation was.

November 9, 1943:

On chain gang digging ditches until they proved they were not guilty.

November 9, 1943, card back:

Well I was still on the chain gang today. I worked this morning and afternoon digging ditches.

However, we got things straightened out and proved we were not guilty so we don't have to go to the chain gang again.

Aunt Annie was one relative who was to play an important role in the time ahead. Here was probably the last card Ken received from her before shipping overseas.

Card from Auntie Anne, November 7, 1943:

We are thinking and praying for you constantly. Glad the crew has one teetotaler anyway keep true and pray.

Presume that the last four days here, your nerves are all upset. Then too with Katy on your mind. You must consider it meant to be whichever way things turn out. If she is serious you will be happy if not don't get too upset – time is a great healer – you will understand more as the days go by.

Chapter 7

On the way to War

Crossing the Atlantic

There was not a lot of information on Ken's trek overseas. Apparently they went down to South America, to Brazil, then crossed over to Africa, and probably flew over the Atlantic just west of Europe to make it to England; they might have flown over parts of occupied Europe at a high altitude or overnight. Altogether, the trip took almost two weeks, but that was not all traveling; there was some down time. The following are some of the places Ken traveled through.

> November 13, 1943, arrived in South America, British Guiana, on way to England.

> November 16, 1943, arrived in Brazil.

While in the States the censors were not that bad, and it was surprising that they allowed some items to be mentioned in letters. But now the crew is going to war and the need for tight security of information is of paramount importance.

> Nov 15, 1943:

> I can't say much due to censorship. We have a pretty good idea where we are going.

Despite the censors, he was able to mention he was in Brazil, along with some information from some soldiers he met while ferrying supplies; without mentioning their names it was probably considered safe information.

> Card with no date:

> I am still in Brazil. We have traveled a good part of the day. It is like Texas a large place so we didn't cover in a day. I am in the plane reliving

one of the fellows from guard duty while he eats. I don't have to stand guard tonight.

November 15, 1943:

We met a couple of fellows last night who had served 22 months with A.V.G. ferrying supplies over the Burma Road. They were telling us various things that happened over there.

The AVG was the First American Volunteer Group.

November 21, 1943, arrived in Western Africa.

November 23, 1943, flew over the Sahara Desert to Northern Africa.

It is of interest that the Air Corps used the southern route—South America to Africa to Europe— to get to England. It seems like a more direct route would have been North America to Greenland or Iceland, both of which were on the Allied side, then to England. Maybe the time of year and weather had an impact or there were other factors which are not readily apparent.

England

Ken's crew arrived in England on Thanksgiving Day, November 25, 1943. While he was never able to communicate his location in his letters home, it is now known that the 448th Bomb group was stationed at Seething, which was about 120 miles northeast of London and about 7 miles from the coast.

Thanksgiving is very much an American holiday so the following passage might seem to be a little confusing, but he was probably referring to Thanksgiving being celebrated on the US bases.

November 25, 1943:

Thanksgiving day, arrived in England too late for the traditional Thanksgiving dinner.

At this point, Ken was very optimistic about when he might return home, however, over the course of the war the number of missions required before rotating home did increase.

November 27, 1943, V-mail:

I expect to be home around August or Sept if everything goes all right as we only have to complete 25 Combat missions. We are anxious to start out on our missions and help get this war over with.

101

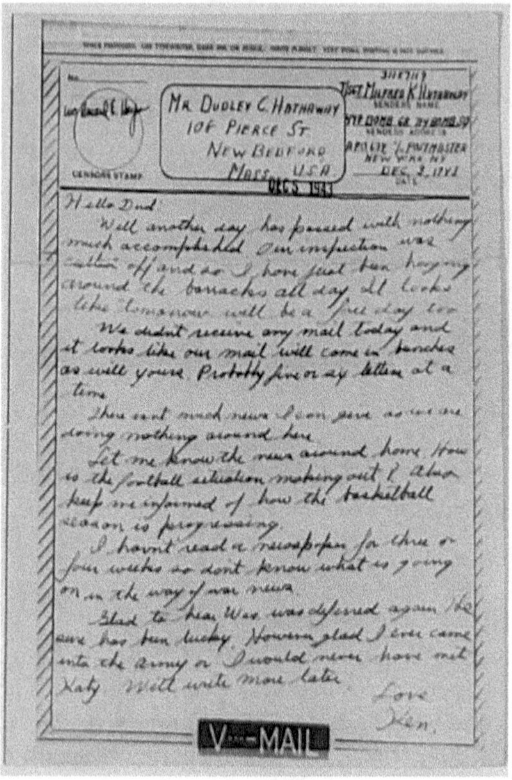

Figure 53. A V-mail letter from Ken.

Some of the mail they received was V-mail, which was an expeditious program used to provide a quicker mail service and to reduce weight for transport overseas. The letters were microfilmed, the film was transported, and then the letters were reproduced and delivered overseas. The entire V-mail letter was often printed in a small size (4x5 inches) and at times almost required a magnifying device to read.

Dec 3, 1943, V-mail:

Well another day has passed with nothing much accomplished. Our inspection was called off and so I have just been hanging around the barracks all day. It looks like tomorrow will be a free day too.

Ken's brother Wes was also in line to be drafted, but he was deferred, delaying his call up.

December 3, 1943, V-mail:

Glad to hear Wes was deferred again. He sure has been lucky. However I am glad I ever came into the Army or I would never have met Katy.

Ken had developed a nice relationship with Katy's parents which is supported by the following passage.

December 8, 1943:

Say tell Ma, Mrs. Babb's birthday is January 15th and I want to send her something. Tell Ma to pick out something nice, even telegraph a nice bouquet of flowers. Anything that would be appropriate and nice for a birthday present. Mail or have it sent to Mrs. Robert Babb and have a card enclosed saying "To Mom from Ken". Don't forget now. I will probably remind you again in a couple of days in case the letter doesn't get through.

It is interesting that Ken is having his mother send flowers to another woman and asking to have "To Mom from Ken" on the card. Even though Ken and Katy were not married or even engaged, Katy's mom referred to Ken as her adopted son.

Christmas card, Mom (Mr. and Mrs. Babb from St. Louis):

How is our adopted son by now? … We think and talk of you a lot, and miss your letters too. Kenneth be sure and go to church and read your Bible & pray. I may tell you we all took a liking to your sis Marjorie. Think she is a swell kid and in many ways like you. Her and Katherine really took in the town. Katherine liked her a lot almost as much as her big brother Ha. Pop – We are still praying for you every day and hoping to see you soon.

It is inevitable that there would be miscommunications that occurred, especially when all the communication was through the mail which always lagged behind a bit. With all the talk of this girl Katy from St. Louis, and Ken even calling Katy's mother Mom, it is probably not surprising that some conclusions were inappropriately reached.

Card dated 1943 from Jeanne:

I also hear you are engaged to the girl in St. Louis. Congratulations!

While the previous miscommunication might seem funny or embarrassing, when miscommunication happened in the military it was a problem that sometimes led to serious consequences. In the passage below Ken and his crew foolishly listened to a rumor of a canceled meeting and got reprimanded for not attending what had been a required meeting.

December 8, 1943:

How's everything going with you. Today was an off day for us and I don't mean maybe, everything went wrong.

We were supposed to get up at 5:00 A.M. but nobody woke us up and we started off wrong by getting up an hour late. We had a meeting which we attended. We then had the morning off.

We were supposed to go to a meeting at noontime but didn't go as heard it had been called off. We sure made a mistake in not going. Your brother almost became a Buck Private and permanently grounded. At that our crew spent two hours on the chain gang digging ditches. They sure don't give a chance for a man to prove his innocence in the Army. He is guilty whether he is or not.

Some of the back and forth between Ken and Dud—the usual banter between brothers—was quite interesting.

December 15, 1943:

I am enclosing our squadron insignia which we wear on our leather flying jacket. What do you think of it? Each squadron makes up their own insignia.

Dud's response in a later letter indicated that he did not think too highly of the insignia.

Figure 54. Ken with his jacket with the squadron insignia.

Now that Ken was in England, he regularly received supportive cards, often encouraging him to keep the faith. Ken had written that he did not think that the letters from home were censored, only his outgoing letters. The first letter seems to support that idea, since it is surprising that news of someone coming close to being a Jap prisoner was not censored.

Card dated 12/15/1943 from Aunt Anne:

Rev. Osborn the missionary is at the Nazarene tonight. Had a narrow escape – came near being a Jap prisoner.

Keep prayed up and let your light shine if you can't go to church. Do the next best go to Chapel services.

Card from Tom Brown, December 16, 1943:

So you are over now in my native land and it is a good country.

You may not have the time or good fortune to find Nazarene Churches over there as you did here, tho there are some, but you should find some good spiritual ones.

I like what you say, that we have so many things to thank the Lord for that we hardly miss a lot of the details. I agree with you and find it so.

Keep looking up, and remember John 14.1 You believe in God, believe also in me. How encouraging it is to know that many of the world's greatest soldiers from Abraham and Moses and Joshua down through to Montgomery, MacArthur, and lots of them were and are real men of God.

12/16/43, V-Mail from Mother:

We had a fine service with Bro. Osborn last night. He certainly went through plenty with the Jap while he was in China. Many a time he didn't know but what he was going to be taken out and shot. He really knew what it meant to be in close contact with the Lord in those days.

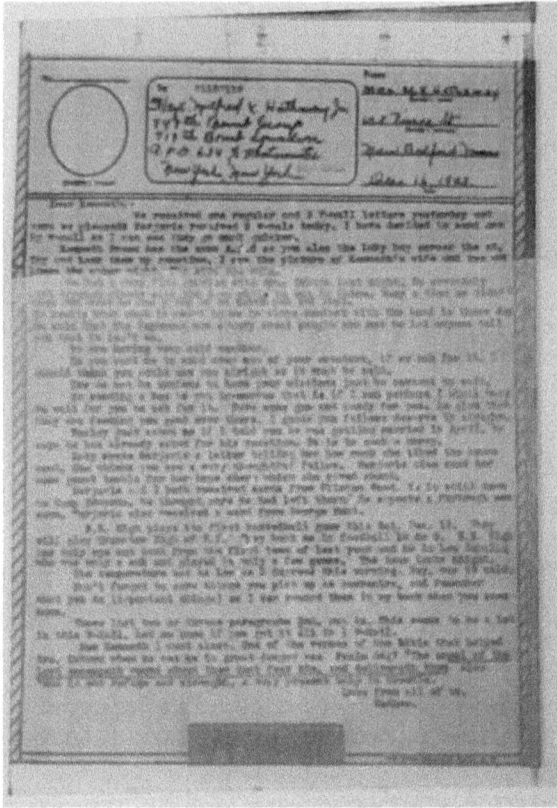

Figure 55. V-Mail from Ken's mother.

Wesley just asked me if I told you he was getting married in April. He says he has already asked for his vacation. He is in such a hurry.

Katy wrote Marjorie a letter telling her how much she liked the house coat. She thinks you are a very thoughtful fellow. Marjorie also sent her some guest towels for her which she raved about.

One of the verses of the Bible that helped Bro. Osborn when he was in great danger was Psalm 34:7 'The angel of the Lord encampeth round about them that fear Him, and delivereth them' also 'God is our refuge and strength, a very present help in trouble.'

Card with no date from Aunt Maude and Uncle Al (1943):

We were glad to hear from you that you are safe in England. You are certainly seeing the world

When you get into action drop one extra bomb for me where it will do the most good (or harm).

106

December 18, 1943, Christmas card from Katy:

It just makes my heart hurt when I think of how lonesome you will probably be on Christmas Day!

Ken was still hopeful about Katy and cards with lines like the last one kept his hopes alive. He tried to make sure that his family sent gifts at Christmas and Valentine's Day that would be from him. It would have been very difficult for Ken to purchase items in England to send back home to the States, so this was one way to ensure that Katy received the items he wanted to send her.

Christmas card from Marjorie 1943:

Well we sent the house coat to Katy and it was beautiful. I sent her a set of guest towels. They are very pretty. We sent them today. I got a letter from her the other day and she said she rec'd some flowers from you and they were beautiful. She said they were all the more nicer and also the card because they came from you. She asked me if I had sent them for you. She said the wording on the card was just right and fit it swell. I guess her boy-friend hasn't come home yet?

In return, Katy certainly did not seem disinterested in the relationship, but maybe just a bit cautious with another boyfriend who was also in the service.

December 21, 1943:

Tell Ma I received two letters from Katy today. In one she said she had written her boyfriend and let me know the details. Even if things don't turn out right for me, although I am inclined to believe they will, I will be glad I sent her the things I have. So continuing sending things I mention until I tell you to stop which I doubt I will ever do.

Ken's brother Dud was always asking about things like the name of the planes on which he flew.

December 21, 1943:

"I don't know how we did come to pick "Chicago Cub" as the name of our airplane. We do have a couple on the plane from Chicago. We first thought of painting a little cub on the plane sitting on a bomb and so decided on "Chicago Cub".

Figure 56. A military themed Christmas card.

December 21, 1943:

Glad you liked the picture of the crew. Thought it was pretty good myself. The 1st engineer is the finest fellow on the crew. I chum around with him more than anybody else. He is married and 21. Has been married a couple of years.

Ken wanted to be able to let his family know when he was going on or had completed a bombing mission, but he knew that the censors would probably eliminate any such mention, so he worked out a code with his family. His Uncle Dudley had been a field clerk in the US Army, had been stationed in Europe, and met and married a German woman whose name was Bertha. So, the plan was when Ken mentioned Aunt Bertha it was a reference to a bombing mission. If the letter fell into anyone else's hands they would have no idea of the bombing mission reference, they would just assume Ken was talking about a family member.

December 21, 1943:

Have received no letters from Aunt Bertha yet so have no news concerning her. Am looking forward to her first letter.

Saying he had received no letters from Aunt Bertha was his way of saying he had not yet been on a combat mission. But he was anticipating his first mission, which, unknown to him, was fast approaching.

Chapter 8

Combat Missions

First Raid – December 24, 1943

Ken went over to England as a part of a bomber crew with the mission to bomb Axis forces. They had been in England for about a month, so it was time for the real missions to start.

Soldiers wanted to be able to let their families know something about their missions and Ken was no different. He had worked out a code with his family to at least let them know when he was going on a bombing mission. The passage below mentions his first letter from "Aunt Bertha". As mentioned, this was the code to tell his family when he went on bombing missions.

December 24, 1943, letter

Mail has just come in and I received a Christmas card from Harriet. I also received my first letter from Aunt Bertha today and everything is fine. Thought you would be interested.

P.S. Katy will probably be interested in knowing I heard from Aunt Bertha as it is the first time I have heard from her so let her know I got the letter.

Biggest U.S. Mission Hits 'Rocket Area'

1,500 Bombers, Fighters Raid France Without A Single Loss

Two thousand Allied warplanes seized air mastery over the invasion coast of France during the Christmas weekend and hammered targets which may have been the Nazi's secret rocket gun emplacements.

The raids, climaxing a five-day assault on installations in the German-held Pas de Calais area, were carried out Friday by some 1,500 bombers and fighters of the U.S. Air Forces, and more than 500 RAF, Dominion and Allied fighters and medium and light bombers.

Not one fighter or bomber was lost from the huge fleet which set up an air umbrella over a deep beachhead along the closest French coast. Luftwaffe fighter planes were unable to get past even the outer fringe of the cordon of Allied fighters surrounding the bombers, and crews in many instances were able to make two runs over the targets to insure accuracy.

1,300 Forts, Libs, Fighters

A force of more than 1,300 Flying Fortresses, Liberators and American fighters made up the heavy artillery of the armada. A big formation of Marauders also went out, while the RAF sent out Mitchells, Bostons and Typhoons to hit similar targets. RAF, Dominion and Allied fighters covered the medium and light bombers.

Figure 57. Start of a newspaper article on Ken's first raid.

● *Washington unofficial military circles last night suggested, says Reuter, that the great Allied five-days-old blitz on the Pas de Calais area is the start of the Second Front "softening up."* SAVE

2,000 Planes Raid 'Rocket' Coast— Not One Was Lost

MORE THAN 2,000 ALLIED PLANES ON CHRISTMAS EVE CARRIED OUT A SUCCESSION OF DEVASTATING BOMBING RAIDS ON THE "ROCKET GUN" COAST OF NORTHERN FRANCE—WITHOUT THE LOSS OF A SINGLE PLANE. IT WAS A RECORD BLITZ.

The U.S. Air Command in Britain alone sent out more than 1,300 heavy and medium bombers and fighters. This armada included well over 500 Flying Fortresses and Liberators, the greatest force of heavy bombers ever sent out to attack a single target. In addition, R.A.F. Mitchells and Bostons as well as Typhoons took part.

'Pre-Invasion Blitz'

The great assault, fifth day of the non-stop daylight offensive against Northern France, went on throughout daylight. Hour after hour the bomber and fighter forces went across the Channel in great processions.

Although the targets have not been officially named, it is believed that German "secret weapon" installations, possibly rocket guns, have been blasted. The U.S. statement that a task force of more than 1,300 planes attacked the Pas de Calais area added that "special military installations" were the objectives.

Unofficial military circles in Washington suggested that the great attacks are the start of the pre-invasion "softening up."

Returning crews on Christmas Eve described the bombing as exceptionally accurate.

An aerial observer who watched the attack through the open bomb bay doors of one of the Marauders

Figure 58. Start of another newspaper article on Ken's first raid.

112

Ken's first bombing mission was to the coast of Northern France in the Pas de Calais area. This was sometimes referred to as "the rocket coast" because it was where the Germans launched V1 and V2 rockets toward England. This raid was the largest force of heavy bombers ever sent out to attack a single target. The newspaper articles in Figures 57 and 58 are a little inconsistent — not unexpected during wartime when specific details are often not available— but it appears that around 1500 fighters and bombers from the United States Army Air Corps (USAAC), joined with over 500 from the Royal Air Force (RAF) in one joint operation. Not one plane was lost on this huge mission, which was definitely noteworthy.

Ken's crew was still flying the "Chicago Cub". The context in which he hoped to get a newspaper to mention the "Chicago Cub" is unclear, but I would assume he was hoping for some significant accomplishment.

December 27, 1943:

The Chicago Cub is doing O.K. and we hope we can get her in the papers sometime.

Second Raid – December 31, 1943

Evidently, they sometimes were aware of upcoming raids. The next passage indicates that Ken would be busy the next day when he wrote this on December 30. The next day was their second raid.

December 30, 1943:

Expect to be busy tomorrow for a change so may have a little more news for you.

1944

Ken confirmed the raid to his family with the Aunt Bertha mention in a letter he sent the next day. Saying that everything is O.K. was his indication that the raid went well; his plane was not damaged, nor was the crew injured.

January 1, 1944:

No mail was received tonight. Uncle Sam is slowing up the last three days. Yesterday I received my second letter from Aunt Bertha. According to the letter everything is O.K. Hope to hear from you tomorrow.

Third Raid – January 4, 1944

Ken's third raid was his first raid over Germany, and it may have been over Kiel, Germany. While not mentioned explicitly in the letter, the crew ran out of oxygen while returning, which may have meant that they needed to drop to a lower elevation where they didn't need oxygen. There was also an indication of how cold it could get with the temperature reaching -60 degrees. Ken evidently tried to communicate some information about the raid, because the letter was censored right after the mention of Aunt Bertha.

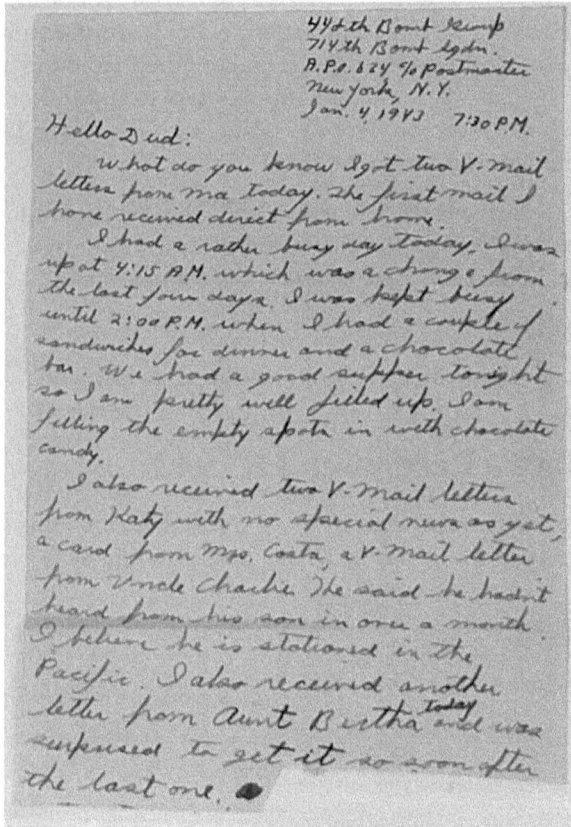

Figure 59. Censored letter from January 4, 1943,
with the bottom portion cut off.

January 4, 1944:

I also received another letter from Aunt Bertha today and was surprised to get it so soon after the last one.

The next few lines were cut out by censors. Sometimes, even without the Aunt Bertha mention, you could tell that Ken had probably gone on a raid. Like when he wrote about starting early in the morning, being busy all day, but making no mention as to what he was doing.

January 4, 1944:

I had a rather busy day today. I was up at 4:15 A.M. which is a change from the last four days. I was kept busy until 2:00 P.M. then I had a couple of sandwiches for dinner and a chocolate bar.

The January 4 mission was a fairly large and successful raid with 371 B-17s and 115 B-24s with an escort of 70 P-38s and 42 P-51s. The total losses were fairly small: 11 B-17s, 6 B-24s, and 2 fighters.

Back home, Ken's brother Wes had gotten engaged and was planning on a wedding in April, though Ken was overly optimistic in hoping to be able to get home by summer.

January 4, 1944:

So, Wes is positive of getting married in April. Tell him he ought to wait. If I am lucky around here I ought to be home this summer, I hope, I hope.

As Ken's interest in Katy grew, the disappointment of Muriel, the girl from his home church, took a troubling turn. Later in life, after the immediate disappointment faded, Ken and Muriel were certainly cordial to one another.

January 4, 1944:

There must be a mistake about Mrs. McKay receiving a Christmas card from me. I didn't send her any. I see they are still trying to cause a bit of trouble or commotion at home over Muriel. I feel real sorry and don't know what I would do if I ever brought Katy home. I sent Muriel a Christmas card also Mr. + Mrs. Gates.

Fourth Raid – January 14, 1944

Ken's fourth raid was again into German-occupied France. Again, he references an early start in the morning, along with a long busy day, but without giving details on a day when he also mentions a "letter from Aunt Bertha".

January 14, 1944:

I had to crawl out of bed at 4:45 A.M. wasn't that awful. We were kept so busy today that I never had any dinner and the only thing that kept me from starving to death was a swell supper we had, in fact one of my favorite meals here, meat pie.

The mail came in a few minutes ago and I received two from Ma dated Jan 1st V. Mail, a card from a girl in Florida, a letter from Betty in St. Louis and last but not least a letter from Aunt Bertha. I had been expecting a letter from her for the last few days as the last I heard from her was on Jan. 4ᵗʰ. According to her letter everything is fine.

Given his last sentence it appears to have been a safe, uneventful raid.

Ken was still trying to win over Katy and others were rooting for him, including her good friend Betty.

January 14, 1944:

I might tell you what Betty wrote about Katy and her boyfriend, quote, 'Ah! While I think of it Delton is home on a furlough. He came in Fri evening and has to leave next Sunday. I kept teasing Katy and asking if she had made up her mind yet. I'll let you in on a little secret, I'm keeping my fingers crossed for you. Katy's getting prettier every day. Hurry home, so you can help her make up her mind.' I see I have one person in St. Louis pulling for me anyway, I didn't hear from Katy today but expect the next letter to probably tell the tale.

Through it all, Ken's faith remained strong and steadfast.

January 14, 1944:

P.S. Never a day goes by but what I read the Bible and thank the Lord in prayer for his protection.

January 19, 1944:

Thanks for the verse you put on the end of your letter. I really appreciate it.

I will say of the Lord, 'He is my refuge, and my fortress, my God, in Him will I trust.'

There was often a bit of playful banter between Ken and Dud. Ken had explained the squadron insignia for the 714ᵗʰ and Dud cleverly pointed out a few issues with it. I don't know what all the issues were, but at least one had to do with the fact that the bomb used in the insignia appeared to be a torpedo, which was not the type of bomb Liberators dropped. Torpedoes were exclusively used to sink naval vessels, which again was not the type of bombing expected in the European Theater of Operations. But even in the midst of the back and forth ribbing of siblings there was often a seriousness because of the severe circumstances.

Figure 60. The 714th Squadron insignia.

January 21, 1944:,

So you are criticizing our squadron insignia are you. I am only teasing you. It isn't too bad although you might be right on the torpedo idea.

You don't have to worry about sending me clippings on crashes. We have become hardened to that; in fact we have to after being in combat it isn't easy to lose your buddies and come back to empty beds in the barracks. If we started thinking about it and letting it bother us our nerves would surely crack.

The various airplanes could take a significant beating but still fly and return home. For the crews this was a bright spot. Yes, they were performing a dangerous duty, and some would not make it home, but the planes they flew in were tough and able to fly even after taking quite a bit of damage.

January 22, 1944:

I am enclosing quite a few clippings which are very interesting. None of them have any reference to anybody I know of but I sent them to show what punishment these planes can take.

Despite logging significant time in the air, Ken did, on a couple of occasions, get air sick. Luckily it was not on a combat mission.

January 22, 1944:

Well this morning I was up at 7:30 A.M. and we had one of our usual swell breakfasts. At 8:30 A.M. was told we were to go up for a short hop.

117

I'll bet you can't guess what happened. It doesn't seem possible. I got sick. We hadn't been up over ten minutes when I took sick and it was a good thing we were only up an hour as I had all I could do to prevent myself from throwing up. I haven't been as sick as that for a long time. On top of that I had pain above my left eye. It must be from a cold I have caught the last couple of days which affected my sinuses. I didn't eat any dinner I felt so rotten although I did manage to sample their dessert which was chocolate cake and it was good too.

These first four raids came over a period of about 3 weeks, but this would not be too typical to have four missions in such a short period of time. On the other extreme, the time between Ken's fourth and fifth raid was an unusually long stretch.

January 22, 1944:,

Have been looking for another letter from Aunt Bertha. Will probably get one within the next two or three days. Will let you know when I do.

Katy may not have made up her mind as to whom she preferred of the two soldiers courting her, but she did continue to send Ken cards and letters.

January 22, 1944, Valentine's card from Katy:

Since you can't tell how the mail is going to be delivered I am mailing this plenty early as you should get it ahead of time.

Did you happen to notice the two blondes on the front? Sorta fits in don't it? And I like the verse too. I think it fits to a T.

So are you gonna' be my Valentine or not? Love Katy

Ken continued to have his family send items to Katy.

January 25, 1944:,

In case my letter of a couple of days ago doesn't get through tell ma to send Katy a bouquet of flowers for Valentine's Day and a nice box of chocolate in a heart shaped box also a nice card like you sent at Christmas time. I can't get anything over here. ... Katy loves flowers that is why I thought it would be nice to send them. I couldn't think of anything else and her birthday is in May. I want to send something real nice then. Also Easter I want a nice corsage sent with a card. Don't forget now. It is too bad I can't get things over here to send but it is impossible.

I haven't any news as I haven't been doing anything. Did I tell you that yesterday we bought a mascot for our crew. A little white dog and we have named him "SALVO". Can you guess why? We are having a hard time house breaking him. Have you any suggestions. Ha.

Salvo did not remain their mascot for very long. A later letter indicated that they got rid of him on January 31, 1944. The difficulty in house breaking the puppy probably led them to return the dog.

It is not clear exactly what the accommodations were for lodging at the base in Seething, but this next note indicated that clearly they did not like having to move back to the barracks.

January 25, 1944:

Woe is me. I'll bet you can't guess what happened this afternoon and are we mad. We are just boiling over. Well about 4:00 P.M. we were told we had to move out of our room and go back to the barracks we were in. I honestly believe the Army hates to see anybody satisfied at all. We put up an argument to no avail and finally moved. It took us until chow time to move.

There were regular USO shows to entertain the troops and the following passage is one show that Ken described in detail.

January 28, 1944:

I tried to rush out that letter last night to Wes as it was late due to my going to the USO show.

Will explain the show a little more in detail. It started at 6:30 P.M. First on the program was a red headed girl who danced and I believe sang a song, next the master of ceremonies kept us laughing with his jokes and witty remarks, then he introduced the girl he said poses for Philip Morris Cigarettes. She was a real brunette and not bad looking. After singing a couple of numbers she came down off the stage and dragged a fellow out of the front seat up on the stage with her. He was real bashful. He broke away from her once but she caught him again. She put her arms around him and started singing. He was getting quite red. Finally she closed her song and kissed him right on the forehead. She had plenty of lipstick and left a beautiful print of her lips on his forehead. It was sure funny. After that they had a comedian with a dummy on his lap. He was very good. The master of ceremonies then imitated a number of well-known celebrities in the radio and screen world and he was good. It closed with a couple of dancers. It sure was a good show, and broke up the monotony around here.

Another correspondence follows, in which Ken is telling his brother about the dates he heard from Aunt Bertha, letting his brother know the days on which he went on raids.

January 30, 1944:

You asked when I heard from Aunt Bertha. I heard from her on Dec 24th and Dec 31st. Then I received one from her on Jan 4th and Jan 14th. Will probably hear from her in the next couple of days and will give you any news of interest.

Ken was still very serious about Katy, as he told Dud.

January 30, 1944;

Haven't heard any definite news from Katy, in fact haven't received any letter from her in four days. She has probably switched from V-mail to regular mail and there will be a delay for a few days. She sure is a swell girl and I hope I can make her your sister-in-law when I get back.

Fifth Raid – February 4, 1944

This had been the longest stretch between raids, 21 days. Ken's fifth raid, which was over Western Germany—possibly Frankfort—was a bit more challenging, and it appeared their plane and crew had a very close call with probably a few flak holes in the aircraft. The mention of Aunt Edith's boy is also interesting, because Ken did not have an aunt named Edith, but Ken's mother went by her middle name, which was Edith. So that may have been a way of talking about his experience without letting the censors know he was referencing himself.

February 4, 1944;

I had a busy day today and am tired. I was up at 4:45 A.M. and was kept busy until 3:00 P.M. I didn't get any dinner except for a bar of candy but made up for it at supper. We had steak, chili, peas, string beans, bread jelly, oranges, cocoa.

Also received a letter from Aunt Bertha today, the first one in 21 days. Everything is fine although she mentioned Aunt Edith's boy got quite a scare. A couple of his good friends had a close call and he was with them.

Write Katy about Aunt Edith's boy as she knows him. Can't give all the details as the censor cut out most of his letter and so Aunt Bertha couldn't give all the details. Seeing as you know the kind of work he is doing you no doubt can guess why he was scared. I can take a good guess. He will probably get used to it.

This mission was also the one in which Ken qualified for the Air Medal. The Air Medal was established by President Roosevelt on May 11, 1942. Over the years, the criteria for earning this medal have changed, evolved, and varied not only by the year, but also by the theater of operations during World War

II, and it even varied by the aircraft flown. The criteria during war time were sometimes lower than during times of peace. For Ken, this medal was awarded for having completed five missions. Not everyone in the crew earned the Air Medal at this time; some of the crew had missed some missions and had not yet reached mission number five.

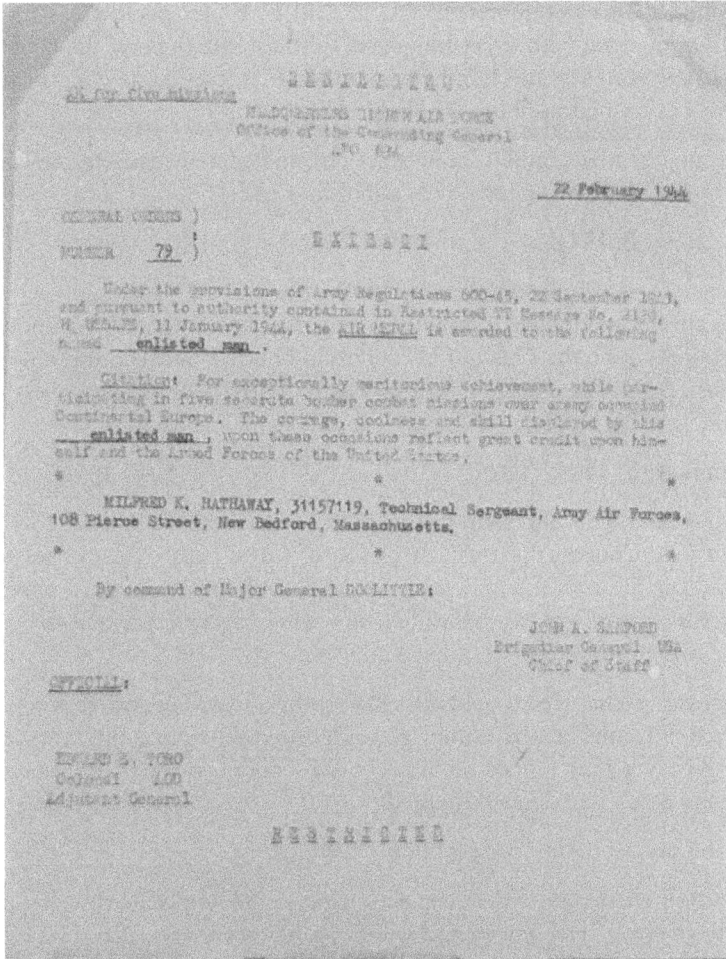

Figure 61. Letter indicating that Ken was awarded the Air Medal.

February 11, 1944:

In case you didn't receive my letter of a few days ago, I earned the Air Medal along with seven others on my crew. It will no doubt be awarded to us in a couple of weeks. Will let you know when it is awarded to us.

Ken was able to make it into London for a short break and was able to tour a few sights.

121

February 6, 1944:

Well here I am in London. I am sitting on my bed in the hotel and thought I would drop you a line before hitting the sack.

February 7, 1944:

I tried to get a kerchief for Marge and Katy but couldn't as they are rationed along with everything else. I did ask the price of them and was told between $15 and $25 for one, and I am not kidding either. I thought she was trying to sell me the store.

My engineer and myself are in the room, and a fellow from an anti-aircraft division. We invited him up to talk things over.

February 8, 1944:

Went to Westminster Abbey, by the House of Parliament and over Westminster Bridge. Also went to St. Paul's Cathedral and under the ground where the Duke of Wellington is buried. Went to the top of the Cathedral and around Whispering Gallery and where the King and Queen are.

February 9, 1944:

Up at 9:00 A.M. and went to the castle to see them change the guard, the Catholic Church, the Bank of England, Royal Exchange and ate where the "Big Shots" eat, after eating we went to the tower and saw where the Dukes, Kings, etc. are beheaded, and where various princesses, queens, etc. were murdered.

It was a shame that Ken would miss his brother's wedding, but that is part of the price those in the active military paid, especially during the time of war. While Ken probably wrote his brother Wes about as much as his brother Dud, very few letters were preserved.

February 10, 1944, letter to Wes:

I am sure enjoying myself traveling around the world. I am seeing things I have never seen before and will probably never see again. It is a lot of fun.

Hope you are able to get deferred again. You sure have been lucky so far.

It is too bad I couldn't be home for your wedding; however, I wish you all the luck and happiness in the world. I don't blame you for not putting it off as I may not even get home this year although I am sure looking forward to it.

Yes if the coast is clear there is no doubt, as far as I am concerned but what I will get married when I get home. She is the finest girl I have ever met and I fell for her right off the bat. I am crazy about her. I don't know just how things will turn out but whatever way it turns out I believe it will be the Lord's will. I have been praying about it and so has she.

I didn't get up until 9:30 A.M. and then read my mail as I had quite a bit of it, two real letters from Katy, one 14 pages and one 12 pages.

Being a teetotaler, Ken did not fit in with some of the others, and the following is a fairly humorous story about his teetotaling ways.

February 10, 1944:

There was an incident that occurred that was quite funny and yet it wasn't. It shows what some of the girls over here think of the yanks. The two fellows I was with wanted a drink and wanted me to come in and wait for them. I didn't want to but as it was partly a restaurant too thought I would. We sat down and one of the girls came up. They said two beers. The girl turned to me and I said," nothing." The girl said to the two fellows, "Is he sick." They said, "He doesn't drink." She looked at me and "Don't you drink," and I said "no." She said "and you are a yank and don't drink." It struck her as so funny she pointed me out to all the girls in the place and I could hear her say, "There is a Yank who is sitting over there that don't drink." I sure was the subject of conversation around there for a while. At least they know there is one Yank that doesn't drink any way. It is too bad there isn't more.

While crews often flew the same plane regularly, sometimes they flew different planes. In some cases, it might have been because of crew illness or damage to the plane which needed repair. Ken flew in a number of different planes, though he had only gone on five missions at this point, so some of these might have been training or practice flights over England.

February 11, 1944:

I might say we don't fly in the "Chicago Cub" any more. It is no longer our plane. We are one of the lead crews here and fly another plane. We have been flying in one lately that is named the "Feather Merchant". We have also flown in "Caroline Chick".

This next passage has a serious tone about the impact of actually being in combat. The reference to Aunt Edith is again interesting, but this was a way for Ken to share information about his recent experiences.

February 11, 1944:

At times it is tough over here, but on the whole not so bad. I was talking with Aunt Edith's boy in London and on his last mission his plane came back with quite a few flak holes in it, however nobody was hurt which is the main thing. The crew was pretty scared for a while he said. It sure is a life of excitement over here anyway. You never know what is going to happen.

From Ma's letter your ambition is to fly. It is all right but not in war time. It is definitely no fun over here although exciting and I hope you never have to see combat in a plane. When you see those ack-ack shells bursting around you, you're just scared and that's that. I still love to fly though and it just gets in your blood after a while.

The Aunt Bertha code had one challenge and that was that Aunt Bertha was still around and married to Ken's uncle Dudley. At times Ken needed to distinguish which Aunt Bertha he was referring to.

February 11, 1944:

Yes I received the card from Aunt Bertha on Ocean St. and wrote her a letter. I didn't want you to get her mixed up with the other Aunt Bertha. I haven't heard from Uncle Dudley's wife (Bertha) since last Friday. Am due to hear in the next couple of days.

So Ma doesn't think I should plan on Katy too much. Well I am not too much but somehow feel pretty certain things will work out all right. I don't blame her for holding on to him after all I am in combat and he isn't. She is in a tough spot and I will wait and see how things turn out.

Delton, Katy's other boyfriend, was in the military but not in a position that put him in combat.

Earlier Ken had been very optimistic that he might be home by summer, but the reality was sinking in. The criteria for going home changed and he now needed 30 missions. He had been there for over two months, yet had only completed five missions; his time frame of getting home was constantly revised.

February 11, 1944:

I hope May is right in that the war will end in July. However, in connection with my being home by Christmas, here's hoping. At first I thought I would be home by my birthday and then I figured at least by Christmas, but now I wonder. I am afraid I may get hooked for an instructor over here. However, I will be willing to stay as an instructor on the ground if I can finish my tour over here. A ground job over here isn't bad. Of course I would rather come back to the States and am going to figure out all the angles on how to get back when I finish up my flying over here.

Ken was mentioned in a Boston paper and it surprised him.

February 12, 1944:

Will now answer your letter of Jan 28th. Say I was sure surprised at hearing my name was in the Boston paper. I am getting up in the world. Ha. One of the fellows has borrowed the piece as his pilot's name is Lt. Conrad whose picture is on the piece. Lt. Conrad's crew sleeps right next to our crew here in the barracks. The file mentioned in the ████████ I know a couple of the fellows involved in the accident although no one was hurt which is the main thing. The plane was ███████ and is still ███████

Given how strict the censors were, it is a little surprising that they did not redact the following passages that included a number of crew names, although they removed confidential information from parts of the last portion. .

February 12, 1944:

The ones that have been going to church are Mel Schefelbein, our tail gunner, Randy Laing our nose or lower turret gunner and sometimes Brown the engineer and myself. We also have three fellows from another crew that go with us.

I might say Lt. Conrad is a swell pilot and I know him very well. I have flown with him in the states. Lt. Doherty whose picture is there was my Communication Officer in the states. He is a swell fellow and we all like him. He helped a lot in getting my Staff Sergeants rating. He tried two or three times to get it for me before I did get it.

As I said before this clipping refers to my base here. I didn't see this particular accident happen ███████ I know most of the fellows mentioned but not by name. I know Erban quite well and talk with him once in a while. Jon A. Beauliese is in my barracks. He is a fairly new fellow. He replaced someone missing in action. John J. Daley goes to church every Sunday with us. He is one of the old gang in this outfit. I know quite a few of the others but not very well. I was surprised to see our ███████ mentioned in the paper.

Sixth Raid – February 13, 1944

Ken's sixth raid occurred on February 13 and was over northern France. Their crew was one of the top crews in his squadron, which meant they were often a lead plane in the bombing formation. When communication was needed, it was probably busy, important, and maybe even frantic, but much of the time they were on radio silence so as to not give anything away.

February 13, 1944 (taken from notes he kept rather than included in a letter home):

Failed to write home for the first time since arriving in England. Went to church in the morning. Following dinner, which was only a sandwich and canned pear, went on our 6th raid to Northern France. Got quite a few flak holes and hydraulic system was smashed so we had to make an emergency landing at an R.A.F. field. The R.A.F treated us royally. After supper went over to a building where four or five of them were sitting around chatting. Beer was served but I had lemonade. Fixed our plane the next day and came back to our field.

February 18, 1944:

I am on one of the lead crews of our squadron. We don't have too much work to do over here. We keep radio silence on all missions except in case of an emergency or special messages.

The censors seemed to vary a bit between different units, which is probably not too surprising; different individuals would be making the call as to what was or was not appropriate to include in correspondence with those in the US. Ken seemed to think that their censor was stricter than others, but the following passage provides a fairly large amount of military information.

February 13, 1944:

Was reading Aunt Bertha's letter of Feb 4th and she was telling about Roger who used to work for Mr. Dunham. I believe you knew him didn't you. Well he is over here in Heavy Bombardment. He must have come over here about the same time I did by the way he spoke. He said he went on one fairly rough mission and that it got around 40 below zero which isn't unusual. When they landed at their field he counted between 20 and 25 flak holes in the plane. No one was hurt however, which is the main thing. If I can get his address will look him up. I often wonder why in some groups they can write more than we can. Some can even tell when they have been on a mission and little details that have no value for the enemy. They are very strict here with us.

Besides Katy, Ken had other admirers from back in the states. Esther was a woman he had met while he was stationed in Sioux City, IA and with whom he corresponded, as he wrote to his brother Dudley.

February 13, 1944:

P.S. …also two letters from Esther in Sioux City. I will have to watch by the way she writes she wants to go steady with me. Oh me. Oh my. I also received another one from Katy dated 2/5, I hear from her all the time now.

There were times when communication to family and friends did not reach its intended destination. Sometimes it was a consequence of the war, while other times there might have been more personal reasons. Ken had sent a Christmas card to Muriel, his friend from his home church, but she never received it. Ken suspected that her parents intervened, wanting to keep their daughter from thinking more seriously about Ken than she should, to keep her from being disappointed or hurt.

February 13, 1944:

So Muriel didn't receive any Christmas card from me. It looks like her folks saw to that. Well it is just one of those things. I sent her one anyway.

P.S. Was just informed by the Post Office a boat was sunk carrying a lot of packages and letters for us. Maybe that is why I haven't received any from you. I'll get even with Hitler for that on my next raid, you wait and see.

Ken was evidently able to get a pass for a few days. He even got to attend and speak at a very small Nazarene church.

February 19, 1944:

Left at noon and went to Leeds, England. Got there at 11:00 P.M. Got a place to sleep at about 2:00 A.M.

February 20, 1944:

Got up at 8:30 A.M. and went to the Nazarene Church. 15 out to Sunday School. 5 out for church service. Went to pastor's house for dinner. Went to another Sunday School program in the afternoon and there were 40 out. Evening service was from 6:30 P.M. to 8:00 P.M. Ten out at night. I spoke about 15 minutes.

Seventh Raid – February 25, 1944

Ken's seventh raid was over Germany on February 25. As he wrote to those at home, there was at least one crew to whom he referred to as a close friend, but who did not make it back from the mission.

February 26, 1944:

When I got back to the barracks I found a swell letter from Katy. It certainly put morale up 1,000%. She said she was down to the USO as they were having open house. While there she saw a blonde fellow that looked like me. She couldn't keep her eyes off him and she hardly slept a wink all night. She seems to worry a lot about me.

I heard from Aunt Bertha yesterday with some sad news. She seems quite broken up about it. Some very close friends of hers were going out for a ride. She saw them in the morning but at night received news they had an accident and all the results are not known. Some were killed and by the way she spoke there is not much hope for the others in the car. Aunt Bertha seems to be O.K. and her own family though.

Continue to remember us in prayer as we sure need it.

Things with Katy seemed to be turning in Ken's favor.

February 29, 1944:

Well I guessed wrong in yesterday's letter on the amount of letters I would receive tonight. I did get the most important one though from Katy. I didn't hear from you or Aunt Bertha. Mail is very light tonight so will get the two I missed tonight (or) tomorrow.

I really received a swell letter from Katy tonight and it looks like Delton is losing a very close battle. If only I could get back to see her soon. Here in part is what she wrote:

> Just picture me without you and you without me,
>
> Just close your eyes and you'll see
>
> How lonesome we'd be.
>
> Skies would fall stars would all tremble
>
> Life would be out of time, dreams would soon crumble,
>
> There'd be no me without you, no you without me.
>
> And yet nobody could be as happy as we,
>
> Smiling through, always together
>
> I can't picture me without you.

How's that? It sounds pretty good to me.

My trust is in the Lord more than ever and I know only He can bring me back.

Keep praying for us, we need your prayers.

Eighth Raid – March 2, 1944

Ken's eighth raid was on March 2 over Germany, possibly Frankfort again.

March 3, 1944:

I haven't done much today. I didn't get up until 10:00 A.M. as I was pretty tired from yesterday.

I did receive a letter from Aunt Bertha yesterday or did I tell you last night.

The raids were having a positive effect, as indicated by the following, though Ken had not gone on the raid referenced.

March 3, 1944:

The item, 'Nazi output Fighter Cut to Ribbons' was out of Monday's paper and has reference to the mission Friday that the 8th Air Force made.

Expect also to hear from Aunt Bertha by Sunday, if not these letters will have to wait until Thursday as I have a two-day pass starting Monday. I haven't definitely decided whether to go out or not. I may go to Birmingham but it takes so long to get there.

Ken's family did not know where in England he was, but that did not stop his younger brother Dud from trying to figure it out. Previously, Ken had written about trying to decide if he should go to Leeds or Birmingham, so Dud assumed that Ken was somewhere between these two cities. That was good reasoning, and while Ken was a similar distance from each of these two cities, he was actually quite a bit further east near the coast.

March 4, 1944, letter to Ken from Dud:

I have before me a map of England. I have found Leeds and I see it has a population of about 482,789 or more than 4 times the size of New Bedford. Judging from your question as to whether to go to Leeds or Birmingham, I take it you are stationed between the 2 cities somewhere maybe near Mansfield, Nottingham, Derby Lincoln, Sheffield, Carlton, Rotherham, or somewhere near there. How's my guess?

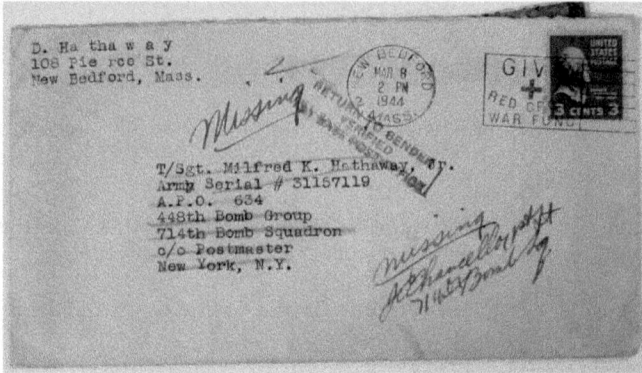

Figure 62. Letter returned to Dud because Ken's plane had gone missing. Dud mailed the letter on March 8, 1944, but by the time it reached England Ken's plane was missing.

One reason this letter from Dud to Ken was preserved was that it was returned to sender when Ken' plane did not return on a later mission.

In his letter Dud included encouraging words, and on several occasions, poems he had written.

March 4, 1944, letter to Ken from Dud:

Ken, the Lord is surely protecting you and I hope you don't forget to thank him for his goodness to you. I have put my trust in Jesus and I feel sure that if you keep looking to Him He will bring you through.

Well it is getting late and I have some things to do yet so I will close with this short poem.

THIS I KNOW

I know not by what methods rare,

But this I know, God answers prayer.

I know that He has given His word,

Which tells me prayer is always heard.

And will be answered, soon or late;

And so I pray, and calmly wait.

I know not if the blessing sought.

Will come in just the way I thought,

But leave my prayers with Him alone,

Whose will is wiser than my own

Assured that He will grant my quest,

Or send some answer far more blest.

So long and may the Lord Bless You, Dud.

Ken continued to let Dud know about various aspects which he assumed Dud would be interested in.

March 10, 1944:

I didn't hear from Aunt Bertha but expect to tomorrow night. I am due to hear from her again.

After eating I went over to headquarters and got my Air Medal. It is a nice looking medal and I am going to try and send it home Air Mail within the next day or two. I then went down to the dispensary to get a shot. We are due to get them again. There was such a big line I didn't bother to wait.

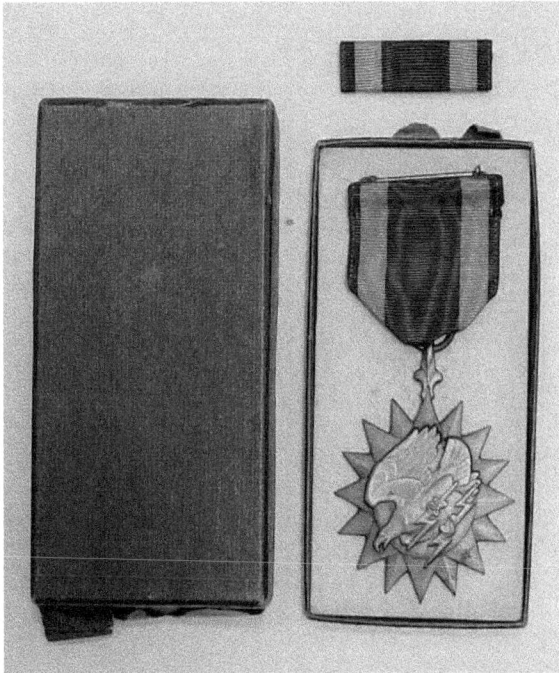

Figure 63. The Air Medal awarded for completing five combat missions.

That is strange that Billy McKay's mascot was named "Salvo" too. We named ours that because on our first couple of missions we had to salvo our bombs out instead of toggling them out, one by one. The reason you gave wouldn't have been far from wrong though.

131

The clipping about the Lib named "No Name Jive" is interesting in that I flew a mission in that plane.

In one letter Dud inquired as to whether Ken was at the same base as Jimmy Stewart.

March 10, 1944, letter from Dud:

By the way are you at the same Liberator base as Jimmy Stewart the actor? The reason I ask is this. Shortly after you landed in England I heard over the radio that Stewart had landed in England. He also left from Sioux City, Iowa. He is now a major in charge of a Liberator Squadron of 15 bombers and had eight missions to his credit. He has just been awarded the Air Medal.

Jimmy Stewart was not at the same base, he was in the 445th Bomb Group, while Ken was in the 448th Bomb Group. Ken's group was in Seething, while the 445th Bomb Group was in Tibenham, about 8 miles west southwest of Seething.

The mental and emotional impact of the war was tremendous and affected all the soldiers. They may have put up a brave front, but in letters back home to family and close friends, the real emotions sometimes came out.

March 3, 1944:

In the clipping of the Forts riding through the flak, it gives a good illustration of the flak bursting around. I dread that more than anything else.

March 10, 1944:

Sometimes I wish I had never seen a plane and I am not kidding. I mentioned to Katy that I might apply for Aviation Cadet and she said "No" with a capital "N". I told her when I got back if she answered a certain question with a three letter word I would quit flying as much as I really love to fly. I sure hope you never have to get in this war, it is no fun.

It is hard on you seeing your buddies killed and after wondering how you are going to make out on the next one. Taken into consideration all I have said I still think you are as safe up in the air as on the ground.

March 11, 1944:

Sure wish this war would hurry up and end. I am getting tired of it. Maybe we can finish them off this year. Here's hoping.

Ninth Raid – March 13, 1944

Ken's ninth raid was over France again and apparently went quite well, so well in fact that he did not mention Aunt Bertha until he was several lines into the following letter. He did continue to thank the Lord for His protection though.

March 13, 1944:

I also received Ma's letter of Feb 29th, a letter from Esther, one from Kaplan's and one from Betty in which she said, 'I'm hoping with all my heart you win (having reference to Katy) but she is the one that has to make up her mind between you two soldiers but I'll suggest to her a little along too. I think her mom & pop are working along with us too.' How does that sound? It sure sounds good to me. I almost forgot I received one more letter from Aunt Bertha and it contained good news, much better than the last few. Everything is going along fine with her.

The Lord certainly has been good to me over here and I praise him for it. He has protected us and I believe He will continue to do so.

While Ken had his heart set on Katy, there continued to be interest from other girls.

March 13, 1944:

Yes I received a swell Valentine card from Katy and thought I wrote you about it and wrote the verse out.

I am not letting the situation with Esther get too serious. She sure is serious though. However, she knows I've got a girl in St. Louis I am crazy about because I told her so.

Ken continued to keep Dud updated on various aspects of military life and his experiences.

March 13, 1944:

We not only lost the "Chicago Cub" as a crew but the plane itself is no more. It ran into a little tough luck about a month ago on a mission. It sure was a good plane.

The reason only seven in my crew received the Air Medal is that the other three hadn't completed five missions. They have now though. I think the Co-Pilot just has five.

I don't wear a regular flak helmet. I wear the kind the infantry uses in battle.

March 14, 1944:

You wanted to know the names of the various planes we fly around here. Well here goes a few I have flown in. Of course I have flown in the "Chicago Cub" but only a couple of times over here. I also have been in "Car-O-Line Chick" "Feather Merchant" a couple of times and here is a good one "Sad Sack". Then we have "No Name Jive", how's that one. The last couple of times our plane had no name to it. Incidentally of these I have flown besides a few others I earned my Air Medal in "Feather Merchant".

I sure will be glad when I get the D.F.C. because that will mean my flying days over here will probably be over with. I sure hope so anyway.

Thanks for the poem on "My Prayer", I thought it was good.

March 15, 1944:

I am pretty sure my tail gunner has credit for bringing a plane down. He was flying with another crew that day and they were jumped by fighters. We were not scheduled to fly that day. He is one ahead of us on missions.

You mentioned about Aunt Edith's boy not getting used to the raids. I think he will probably get used to it in a way, although I haven't seen the raid yet I wasn't a little bit worried. It sure isn't any fun.

Ken's mention of the DFC (Distinguished Flying Cross) is a little perplexing. He makes it sound as if he would receive it once his tour of duty was complete, but that was not necessarily part of the criteria for the award. In fairness to Ken, though, the criteria varied depending on numerous aspects including the Theater of Operation, the type of combat, and one possible set of criteria did include completing the assigned missions.

Ken was still trying to read into Katy letters and felt that he was winning the battle for her heart.

March 15, 1944:

No I believe you are wrong in that Katy has decided on Delton. In fact I am almost positive she has decided on me but is waiting until I get back for which I don't blame her. In her letter of March 1st she mentioned going to a wedding and here is what she said. 'It was a church wedding and I have never seen a fellow any more in love than he was. You could see it sticking out all over him. He couldn't take his eyes off the bride. He kept his eyes right on her all the way down the aisle. It was really cute to watch him. I told mom later that if I ever get married I hope my husband loved me that much. You want to know what she said. Well remind me to tell you sometime.

Sure wish I was going to be home for the wedding (Wes's wedding). You can expect to see my bride when I get home on my furlough. I am hoping to bring Katy home for a week if I can.

One unusual aspect of the relationship that Ken had with Katy was the strong connection to Katy's parents. They thought very highly of Ken and considered him an adopted son even though his time in St. Louis was relatively short (about 5 months) and their only real exposure to him was from leaves and passes when he went to attend church or visit some of the young people from the church.

March 15, 1944:

I can almost imagine what mom (Katy's mom) said and I think she told Katy I would be the one to love her that much. She (Katy) told me her folks think the world of me.

Ken continued to thank the Lord for his protection, though he commented that while the rest of his crew was not very religious, he thought they might be praying at certain moments during their missions.

March 15, 1944:

I wish you wouldn't worry so Mom, no kidding, There is no need of worrying about something already happened or getting upset about it. The Lord is protecting me and I believe he will continue to do so.

None of the fellows on my crew are the least bit what I would call religious. However, there is no doubt most of them do a lot of praying when we get in a tough spot.

Flying a lead plane, or deputy lead plane, was a more prestigious role, though it often meant that higher ranking officers were accompanying them on the plane.

March 14, 1944:

In one of Aunt Bertha's letters she was telling me how whenever Paul went on a mission he flew in the lead ship and always had a Colonel, Major, or Captain flying with him. He tried to write who the colonel was but they crossed his name out. If they run it the same as here it was the Group Commander, the Captain generally is the squadron commander. I don't know who the Major would be.

Chapter 9

Mission 10/ Friedrichshafen, Germany

The 10th mission would be Ken's last combat mission. Here is his description of the day and mission, probably recorded that evening and on the next day in notes he kept while in Switzerland, since it certainly would not have made it through the censors as he wrote it.

March 18, 1944:

Sound asleep. That was the state I was in at 4:45 A.M. on the morning of March 18, 1944. However this was not to last. At 5:00 A.M. I felt a touch on my shoulder and then a voice saying, "Roll out of that sack." It was pitch black outside as I crawled over the side of my bunk and hit the floor. Half of my crew were mostly dressed, while the other half were still deciding whether to crawl out or not. I grabbed my clothes and in about five minutes was fully dressed for my tenth mission (little knowing it would be my last one). We then struggled out of the barracks in one and twos heading for the Mess Hall. We had a good breakfast, fried eggs, cereal, fruit juices, a typical meal before a mission. It was then getting along towards 5:45 A.M. and as the briefing was at 6:00 A.M. we left the Mess Hall and got into a truck waiting for us and was carried down to the Briefing Room.

After getting the rest of our clothes on in the locker room, which included our parachute, heated equipment, Mae West, we went into the Briefing Room to see what our mission was for the day. We waited a few minutes and finally the officer came in and lifted the curtain for us to see the map. You could hear a lot of groans go up when we saw the target, for it was FRIEDRICHSHAFFEN, right on the Swiss border, which was a pretty long flight and meant traveling over Germany for quite a long period of time. We were told to expect around 600 enemy fighters, but

136

only moderate flak. We then left the Briefing Room and headed out to our plane.

Figure 64. Uniform patch for the 8th Air Corps.

We spent about an hour checking over our equipment and finally taxied out into position as take-off time was at 8:00 A.M. We were flying Deputy Lead for the whole Division (2nd) of the 8th Air Force Bomber Command that day which meant we had to be on our toes. It was around thirty below zero as we traveled over enemy territory. In the lead ship was the Colonel and we had the Squadron Commander of the 715th Squadron, Captain Edwards. The lead ship started forward and was lost in the fog before it had hardly left the runway. We then went roaring forward. We climbed through the clouds and finally at around 10,000 feet came out into a perfectly clear and beautiful day. The sun was shining real strong.

We flew around England for a couple of hours getting all the planes into formation. I never saw so many planes in the air at one time in my life. There were over 1,000 of them. Finally, we started climbing to the altitude we were to fly at and by the time we reached London we had our oxygen masks on and were flying at around 20,000 feet. It wasn't long before we were out over the English Channel winging our way towards our target. It is sort of with mixed emotions that we reached the enemy coast, somewhere around the Dieppe area. A feeling of uncertainty, expectation with fear mixed in.

We cut across France without any trouble at all and before very long we could see the Alps in the distance and knew it won't be long before the enemy would open up on us with their ack-ack guns. It was very cold and our oxygen masks kept icing up. Before long we reached our Wing IP and then Group IP and we knew a matter of seconds awaited us before we would be on our bomb run. Up until this time we had seen no enemy activity whatsoever, neither fighters or flak.

As we started down the bomb run I could see hundreds of planes curving around in back of us ready to start on their bomb run too. I got the signal from the bombardier to open the bomb bay doors and so crawled down onto the bomb bay and opened the doors. I could see the city beneath us just as plain as day. As we started on our bomb run the next thing I knew was that they had opened fire upon us and by their first burst which broke right in front of us, about 50 feet, knew we were going to be for plenty of trouble. You could hear the flak going off and that was an indication they were pretty close. The next burst hit our wings and then the next three or four bursts all hit us. I could see the city in flames below us as tons of bombs dropped down on them. One of the bombs didn't let go so I called the Bombardier over the interphone and told him to get that bomb out. He finally dropped it and asked me if I had closed the bomb bay doors yet. I told him, "NO" and that I had no intention of going down and closing them with all that flak bursting around us. I had on my flak suit and was standing on another one.

Figure 65. This picture is from a bombing mission, but it is unclear which mission it is from.

What seemed like hours and in reality was only seconds we ran out of the direct bursts of flak and I could hear the pilot calling the various positions to find out if anybody was hurt. Everyone was all right in the nose, and Brown and myself were O.K. However, I could hear him calling "Pilot to Waist, Pilot to Waist" and no answer. The "Pilot to Tail, Pilot to Tail, come in" and no answer. He then said to the co-pilot somebody must be hurt in the back. Things happened so fast from then on it is almost impossible to keep things in order. Brown came down out of the upper turret like a shot as gasoline was leaking all over the place. We tried to get to the rear of the plane but couldn't, and Childs tried to get to the front and couldn't. Brown went out on the bomb bays and managed to get one leak stopped and we figured we could make it back to our base. Knowing something was wrong at the rear of the plane Capt. Edwards, our acting Command Pilot, and co-pilot started for the rear. He hadn't got far when the pilot called me and asked me to come up in the Co-Pilot's seat as the plane was getting out of control. I crawled up into the seat and endeavored to help him keep the plane under control. Our trim tabs, one rudder and one elevator was shot away and the plane wanted to loop and then go into a spin. It took all of our strength to hold the wheel down.

Finally, Capt. Edwards came back and told us that Miltner was hurt. He didn't say how bad so we thought he had just been wounded in the arm or leg. One of the bursts of flak had busted directly in front of him as we later found out and had knocked him flat, together with the other waist gunner. He was bleeding pretty bad as his arm had a good size hole in it, his legs, his chest and back, together with a bad cut in his neck which we later learned had cut his spinal cord and paralyzed him. By this time gasoline was leaking out all over the plane and after a brief consultation with Brown, the navigator and the pilot, it was decided that with the gasoline leaking out as bad as it was we would only be able to make Paris and then have to bail out. The only other course available was to head for Switzerland and hope the plane did not blowup before we got there.

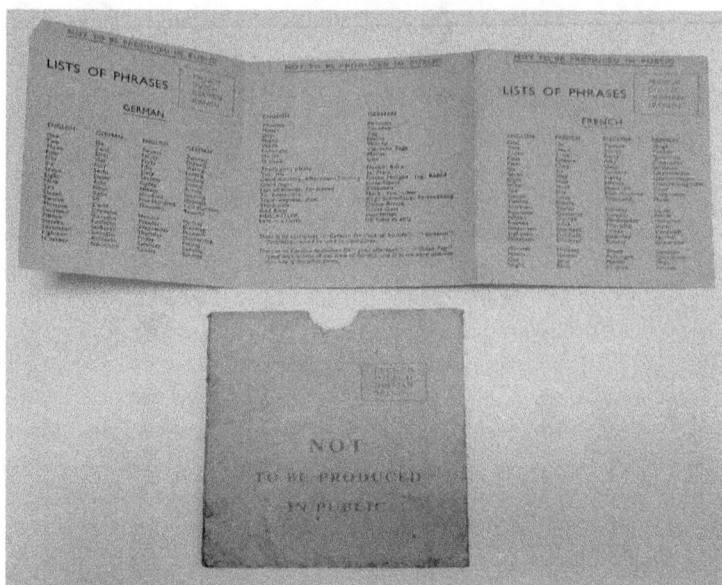

Figure 66. The crews were provided with oilskin maps and lists of phrases in various languages in case they were forced down on a mission.

We left the formation about twenty minutes inside France and headed across the Alps. At first we were going to bail out over Germany, but after another consultation decided we could make Switzerland. I doubt if we would have bailed out anyway considering Miltner was so bad off. We were very much afraid though that we would blow up in mid-air as the gasoline was all over the plane. We finally approached the field at Dubendorf and prepared to land. Just as we were coming in on the runway another plane (B-17) landed right in front of us with two engines out and pancaked on the runway. We had to pick up speed again and go around and then land cross-grain to the runway. We almost ran into about 5,000 people that were watching the planes land and had to put on our brakes real hard. It sure was a good thing that our brakes were working. We had no more then stopped when I went through the upper hole behind my chair out on to the wing and then jumped to the ground. I sort of turned my ankle, which made me limp for a couple of days. I had no more than struck the ground when about five Swiss soldiers surrounded me with raised guns. I didn't move. Finally, I tried to tell one of the men we had an injured fellow in the back. He didn't understand so I said "Ambulance, Ambulance". He understood and went like a shot to get the ambulance which in a few seconds came up to the back of the plane. We were trying to warn the Swiss to stay away from the plane as it might blow up any minute. You could see smoke curling from the superchargers. They took Miltner off to the hospital and little did we know then that we would never see him again.

We were then taken to a building where our maps and compasses were taken away from us and we filled out information sheets for the Military Attaché. After that we were taken to trucks and piled in the back. We were taken to a school in Zurich to sleep overnight as there was no other place large enough to hold us, there were so many of us. There were around 140 of us that day, the largest crowd ever to land in one day in Switzerland. Hundreds of people were following us on bicycles, running, motorcycles and anyway they could. All hollering, "Americaners, Americaners". We finally arrived at the school building and were all put into a couple of rooms with hundreds hanging around on the outside to see us.

Finally around 9:00 P.M. we all decided to hit the sack. Childs said he had been hit in the arm but that it was nothing as the guard wanted to take him to the hospital. However, on undressing we saw that his whole arm was soaked with blood and his clothes. The guard immediately called the doctor and they took him to the hospital. It seems that a piece of flak came through the window, along with about five thousand other pieces and tore a rivet off the plane and put it right through his arm. When we think of it, it is a wonder that all three in the back of the plane as well as the rest of us weren't killed. On looking at the plane after landing there was without exaggerating over two hundred holes from the waist window to the tail of the plane. The whole top of the plane was just as if somebody had taken a can opener and started down the middle of it. Both of Mel's guns were smashed to pieces although he was unhurt. He sure was fortunate. In fact the Lord was with us all.

Later in life, Ken shared very little about his war experience, but he did speak in church one day as a layman in the late 1960s or early 1970s, and shared a few other aspects related to this monumental day.

After getting shot up on the bombing run, the possibility of bailing out was discussed among the crew. In hindsight, we now know about the prisoner of war camps and how Allied airmen and other prisoners were treated, but that was not discovered until the war was nearly over. At this point of the war, there were only rumors and the rumors were that if you were bombing over Germany and parachuted out, you wanted the German military to find you, rather than the local townsfolk. You were bombing their town and the rumor was that the local townsfolk would take downed airmen and hang them on the nearest tree. That may have influenced their decision to not bail out over Germany and to try and make it into Switzerland.

They had to abandon their first approach to the airfield because of the B-17 coming in with engines out. They gained altitude, went around the field again and then landed. But their plane had also lost a significant amount of gasoline, so much so that they probably would not have been able to circle the field a second time. Also of note is that as deputy lead they had been the second plane to take off from England that morning and had been in the air longer than almost all the other bombers on their mission.

Probably the most significant story Ken shared about this mission actually occurred back in the states. One of his aunts, I believe it was Aunt Annie, was in the middle of washing dishes in the morning one day when she suddenly felt impressed to pray, specifically for Ken. So she immediately stopped washing dishes and prayed for her nephew overseas. That prayer happened on March 18 and when you take into account the various time zones, it happened right as they were on their ill-fated bombing run.

God wants us to heed the encouraging of His Spirit and take our concerns to Him in prayer. Prayers do make a difference!

There were some crews and soldiers in the military that looked down on crews who ended up in Switzerland, assuming that they were simply trying to get out of doing their duty—that those crews were more concerned with saving their own skin than serving their country. It is possible that was true for some crews, though it seems unlikely that the entire crew would go along with a fabricated story. In this case, Ken's mission on March 18, 1944, the evidence does not support any questionable motives relating to ending up in Switzerland. The fact that they did the bombing run, and after the run, despite the damage to their plane, headed back toward England and were a ways into France when they turned around to try and land in Switzerland, rather than crash in occupied France, indicates a loyal crew. Also, having Captain Jack Edwards on board, who was the Commander of the 715th Squadron makes the idea of intentionally running from a fight essentially impossible. Probably most of those who ended up in Switzerland were loyal, faithful soldiers who served their country and went to Switzerland because it was the least objectionable option if their plane was so severely damaged that it could not return to base.

Each of the senior staff had to write a report on the mission. Copies of the reports have been listed below. Overall they are very consistent, yet it is interesting to see the different aspects emphasized by the various crew members.

Lt. Carroll's Report on the Mission

Operational Flight March 18. 1944

1. B-24-J

2. No. 284

3. Target: Friederickshaven

4. Take off: 0930. Landed 1545. Bombs Away 1423.

5. Landed Near Zurich with fifteen others.

6. Personnel: Eight O.K.

7. A.E. Childs, Right waist gunner slightly injured by flak.

8. R. F. Miltner, left waist gunner Seriously injured by flak, recovery uncertain.

9. Aircraft: Badly damaged by flak. All gas tanks leaking from wings and into bomb bay. Control cables fouled. Elevator tab inoperative. Oxygen and interphone out from bomb bay to tail turret. All radio equipment, waist guns and tail turret inoperative. 200-300 flak holes on entire ship but concentrated in waist and tail. Four engines and hydraulic system O.K. Landing made without further damage to aircraft.

10. Injured gunner would not have lived for two hours without blood transfusion according to doctor's report.

11. Bad gas leaks make it impossible to estimate remaining fuel.

Robert W. Carroll
1st Lt. A.C.
448th Bomb Group

Lt. Hennessy's Report on Mission

1. B-24-J

2. I

3. 284

4. All fuel tanks leaking, damage to controls.

5. Confidential and secret equipment destroyed.

6. Don't remember. See R. W. Carroll's report.

7. None.

8. Formation went into an intense concentration of accurate flak. Our ship was hit three times before bombs away and one time afterwards. Left waist gunner mortally wounded.

John E. Hennessy
1st Lt. , A.C.
Bombardier

Capt. Edwards Report on the Mission

1. B-24-J

2. 100284

3. Group I

4. Landed in Switzerland because of bad gasoline leaks and a fatally injured man. Damage was done by German flak.

5. There was no further damage after landing. Plane was badly shot up. There were large holes all through the plane, all radios were out, hydraulics out, holes in flaps, and the gas was streaming out of the wings and the bomb bay. All secret equipment was destroyed before landing. Our elevator cables were also shot out.

6. Take off time: 0950.

7. Landing time in Switzerland: 1545

8. Elapsed flying time: 5:55

9. Estimated gas left in tanks, none, balance in tanks ran out on ground.

10. I was riding as command pilot on Lt. Carroll's crew and we were scheduled to fly Deputy Lead in the Group and the 2nd Division. We were the 2nd plane to take off at 0950 from our base in England. Nothing unusual happened on forming the group or the Division, so proceeded on course to our target Friederickshafen. Since we were flying Deputy Lead in the Division we flew on the right wing of the Group Commander, Col. Thompson. We reached our initial point without mishap or any battle damage, and made our run on the target. Bombs went away at 14:25, and at the same time we were hit by several direct bursts of flak which injured our left waist gunner and paralyzed him. Our radios were all dead and we were unable to communicate with the group leader. We had trouble keeping with the formation due to lack of control with the elevators being shot out. We hadn't heard from the men in the back of the plane since being hit by flak, so I went back and saw we were in bad shape. Gas was coming out of the bomb bay and off of the wings.

We stayed with the formation for ½ hour than headed for Switzerland, and landed at 15:45. S/Sgt. Miltner died in Zurich.

Jack P. Edwards
Capt. A.C.
Command Pilot

Lt. Smith's Report of the Mission

1. B-24-J

2. I

3. 284

4. Leaks in all gas tanks, controls damaged.

5. Confidential and secret material destroyed.

6. Do not remember take off. Landed at Zurich 1545.

7. None

8. Formation was fifteen minutes late at target and in order to gain time flew straight across target, did not make sharp turn to right as briefed and encountered heavy accurate flak. Suggest briefed route be followed accurately in target area. We were hit by four separate bursts of flak that tore holes in all gas tanks, shot away elevator controls, destroyed all radio equipment, oxygen system, and waist and tail guns.

Castledon d. Smith
1st Lt., A.C.
Navigator

The crew reports were very consistent, though not perfectly, and seem to represent accurate accounting of the mission, since it is often said it is a sign of collusion if witness reports match too perfectly. The navigator's report is particularly of interest because it indicated how being behind schedule might have played a role in their mission. Their approach to the target did not follow the briefed route, but instead cut across an area which may have contributed to their flying through heavier flak than anticipated. This might have resulted in more damage than if they had proceeded along the originally-planned route.

Chapter 10

Switzerland

Ken's family noticed a stretch when they did not receive any letters from him and were starting to get a little concerned. At least initially, this delay in receiving mail had nothing to do with the mission of March 18, 1943. Instead it was just part of the natural delay in the transportation of the mail from England to the United States.

March 22, 1944, V-mail from Ken's mother:

Have received no mail from you since last Saturday and that was a letter dated March 9th. I did not receive any from the eighth altho' I have received all up to that time. I do hope everything is alright with you.

March 24, 1944, from Dud, returned with "Missing" on the outside of the envelope:

Yesterday we received your letters of 10th, 8th, and 11th. Never in my life was I so glad to hear from anybody. I sure was worried for a while because we had received no mail since the previous Saturday, I just kept on praying and I knew everything would turn out alright. The Lord has sure been good to you. Lately the mail has been very slow. By the way V-Mails are from 1 to 2 days slower than the airmail.

March 28, 1944, V-Mail from Ken's mother:

Just a V Mail today as your mail is very slow coming lately. No mail from you again today. I have more off days than on these days, I didn't receive any letter from you of March 12 altho' I did receive your letter of the 13th yesterday – that was written 15 days ago. I just hope you are O.K.

The letters from Dud always provided an interesting perspective, and often poetry he wrote.

March 24, 1944, letter from Dud:

The only thing that made me disappointed was the fact that you hadn't gone on any more missions. It isn't that I like you to go on missions but when I hear that you have completed another mission safely I feel that it is one more over and one less you will have to do. There's another side to the story though. All the time you are not going on missions somebody is and the Axis is growing weaker and that means that when you do go there will be less opposition.

You keep praying on your end, Ken, and we will do the same on this end. I am sure the Lord will take you through.

> Where is my flying boy to-night—
>
> The boy of my tend'rest care,
>
> The boy that was once my joy and light,
>
> The child of my love and prayer?
>
> O could I see you now, my boy,
>
> As fair as in olden time,
>
> When prattle and smile made home a joy,
>
> And life was a merry chime!
>
> Keep praying my flying boy to-night
>
> Keep praying where you are;
>
> He will protect you through the night
>
> And keep you safe tho' afar.
>
> O where is my Ken to-night?
>
> O where is my Ken to-night?
>
> My heart o'er flows, for I love him, he knows;
>
> O where is my Ken, to-night.

Well, Ken, I haven't much else to say tonight except that we will never stop praying for you. Stand for what you believe, pray for your men, and do the best you can. God hears and answers prayer. Above all don't get discouraged.

P.S. Please pray for me, Somehow I know the Lord wants me for something. I don't know what but I am willing to do what He wants me to do regardless of what it means. As much as I long to fly I will still obey the Lord. Pray for me.

The P.S. in Dud's letter to Ken is interesting. Dud became a pastor after college and eventually joined the Navy as a chaplain. He had a very prominent career as a Navy chaplain and even served for a few years as the chaplain at Arlington National Cemetery in Arlington, VA. He was the last surviving sibling from the family and passed away in 2022. He was awarded the honor of being buried in Arlington National Cemetery.

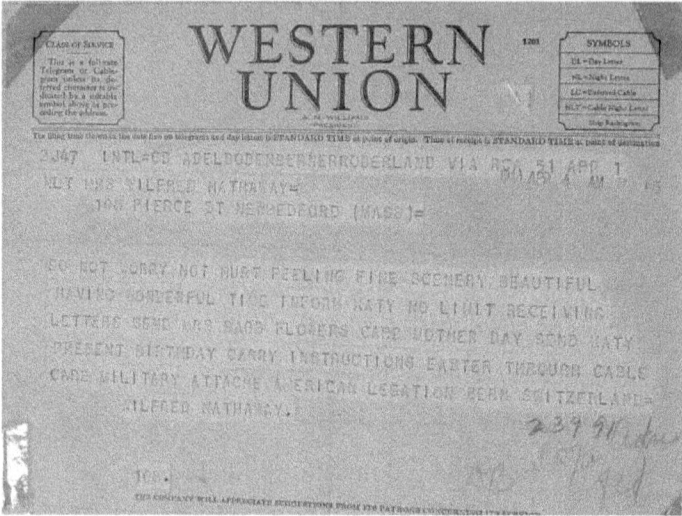

Figure 67. An early telegram sent to Ken's family while in Switzerland.

My understanding is that Ken was able to get communication to his family that he was safe and alive prior to their receiving the official notification that he was Missing In Action. He was able to send them a cablegram, possibly the one shown in Figure 67. With their concern growing because of the lack of mail from Ken, receiving word that he was safe was a blessing. Based on the letter below, it appears that the telegram arrived sometime between April 6 and April 10.

Flyer Interned

MILFRED K. HATHAWAY

Technical Sergeant Hathaway son of Mr. and Mrs. Milfred K. Hathaway of 108 Pierce Street who recently cabled his parents that he is interned in a neutral country, has been awarded the Air Medal. The trophy of his participation in bombing missions over Germany has been sent to his parents here. A former employe in the office of the Hathaway Mill, he was in England for several months before being forced down in a neutral country, presumably Switzerland.

Figure 68. Article on Ken being interned.

April 10, 1944, letter (censored) from mother:

I wrote you a letter on the 6th of April but before I got it mailed Aunt Annie had had hers returned so I knew the address was not correct but the government sent me another address which I will use. I sure was surprised to get a cable from you and needless to say I was a bit excited. I received it at about 8:25 A.M. Marj had not gone to work and I hollered upstairs to her and Wes heard me and came running down the stairs. He stayed around a while and then asked me how the clock happened to stop. I said 'That isn't stopped'. He thought it was noon time. Such a morning as I did have. There was an all-day institute at the W.C.T.U. and I was asked to bring a pie so I had started to make some pineapple pies when the cable came. I was supposed to be there at 10:30. I called up Uncle Al and Aunt Annie. Aunt Ethel called me twice, Aunt Bertha called me that A.M. I called Aunt Edna and then grandpa happened in altho' he had not heard about it. Several spoke of you at the W.C.T.U. and were glad you were safe. Did AUNT Bertha tell you her son had trouble that operation on Mar. 18th. Rev. Brinkman said that the Swiss people are wonderful people. Mrs. Domingues feels that God had a hand in it as do many. You cannot praise him enough. ... Our revival is over. Wesley went up last night also Mrs. Costa and Roy. Wes got through fairly soon but my how they did pray for Roy. Freda cried and prayed and Mr. and Mrs. pleaded and prayed so long. Finally about 10:15 he got up from the altar and walked out. He would not pray through. I understand he wants to be a politician or in the real estate business and the Lord has called him in the ministry... Are the other members of you crew with you, if so tell me who if you can. While I was to church last night a woman called up and wanted to know how I knew where you were ███████ Dad answered and she was to call me to-day but haven't heard from her yet. She lives in Providence ██████ ... Am praying for you and sure will be glad when this war is over and you will be united with us.

You know Wes is supposed to go for his physical on April 27. He will get back from his wedding trip on the 26th.

The Chaplain for the 448th Bomb Group also wrote a letter to Ken's family that seemed to imply the official notification had already been sent to the family, though that was not among the items that were saved in Ken's scrapbook.

Sergeant Interned Following Bombi.

Mr. and Mrs. Milfred K. Hathaway Jr. of 108 Pierce Street have received a cable from their son, Technical Sergeant Milfred Jr., notifying them he is interned in a neutral country following a bombing mission over Germany.

Sergeant Hathaway has been stationed in England for several months participating in missions over Germany as a radio gunner on a B-24 Liberator bomber. He has been awarded the Air Medal and Oak Leaf Cluster. Before entering the armed forces he was employed in the office of Wamsutta Mill.

Figure 69. Another article on Ken being interned aftr a bombing mission.

Letter from Army Chaplain

448th Bomb Group, APO 558
c/o Postmaster, N.Y., N.Y.
April 12, 1944

Mrs. Isabelle Hathaway
108 Pierce Street.,
New Bedford Mass.

My dear Mrs. Hathaway

You have, of course, by this time received official notification that your son, Milfred, is Missing in Action. As a Chaplain with the Bomb Group in which he was serving, I am writing this personal letter to assure you that I join my prayers with yours for his safe return. Circumstances beyond my control have prevented my writing to you sooner

There is a possibility, as you know, that Milfred is at present interned in enemy or enemy-occupied territory. I trust that you will not give up hope that he is alive and well until you have received definite word to the contrary.

Milfred was one of a large force of young men over here who are daily showing a tremendous amount of courage and determination in helping to overthrow an enemy who would destroy everything that we hold dear and sacred. You can be proud of him.

The next few weeks or months will be for you a time of anxiety and great uncertainty—a time when you will long for news or information that will set your mind and heart at ease. I trust that your courage will not fail. You have my deepest sympathy in this time of trouble, and I hope and pray that the life of your son has been spared.

Sincerely yours,
Theodore Runtan,
Chaplain (Capt.)

Ken's ability to send letters home was now greatly curtailed, but he did keep notes as to what the days were like. Much of the remainder of this chapter comes from those notes.

March 19, 1944:

This day was spent hanging around the school building as we could not leave. Crowds hung around all day watching us. We had to walk about a mile to eat and we sure were a spectacle in our flying clothes walking through the streets. We had pretty good meals and spent a good portion of our time trying to fathom German, French, Swiss-German and some

151

Italian, which the various guards spoke. Another good night's sleep was had by all. One of the fellows took off but was caught before he had gone very far.

March 20, 1944:

We were up at 6:30 A.M. as we had to leave to go to our camp. We left Zurich after walking down to the streetcar and taking that to the train. We traveled first class and they sure had some swell seats in the train.

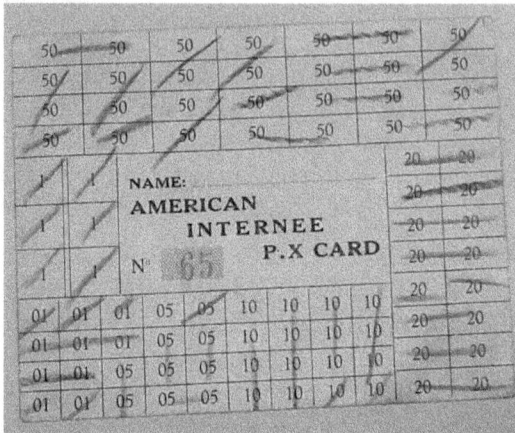

Figure 70. P.X. Card for American Internees.

We found out we were heading for Adelboden which is right in the heart of the Alps, and a very pretty Summer and Winter resort. We arrived at Frutigen around 1:00 P.M. and from there proceeded by automobile up the side of the mountains to Adelboden reaching there at 2:00 P.M. The snow was deep and it sure was a pretty sight seeing the snow-covered Alps from the ground rather than from the air which we had just seen 48 hours before. We were assigned to the Bellevue Hotel which was the newest and finest hotel in Adelboden. We were informed that we were to be quarantined for three weeks, for which time we could not go outside of the hotel except for an hour in the morning and an hour in the afternoon when we took our walks and did any buying at the PX that was needed. We were told we would receive fifteen francs every two days to spend and everything else we bought would be done through the PX and NCO club, where they had cards which they punched on your making purchases and at the end of the month they would add up all the cards they punched and subtract it from your pay. We also had drink coupons and buyer permits which permitted us to go into the stores and buy as much as wanted up to five hundred francs. All we would do is hand them the buyer's permit as payment, after having it signed by the Commanding Officer. The stores would then send the buyer's permits to the Finance Department and receive payment for their merchandise. We were also allowed nine meal coupons per

152

month, which allowed us to eat four meals out or buy cakes and we also received 150 points per month for chocolate, plain or filled. The price of things was pretty high, for example oranges and bananas were ten cents each.

After arriving at the hotel in Adelboden Ken and the others were confined for a few days. One of the crew members, Lt. Robert Carroll, the pilot, even tried to escape but was quickly caught and returned. In a short article published in the April 2000 issue of *The Swiss Internee Magazine*, Carroll shared that he had made several failed escape attempts landing him in various jails, but on January 4, 1945, he finally managed to escape with a Lt. Morris Weinberg, skiing over the mountain to the Lausanne train station, eventually reaching a "safe house".

The letter below was one of the first letters Ken was able to write after he made it to Switzerland.

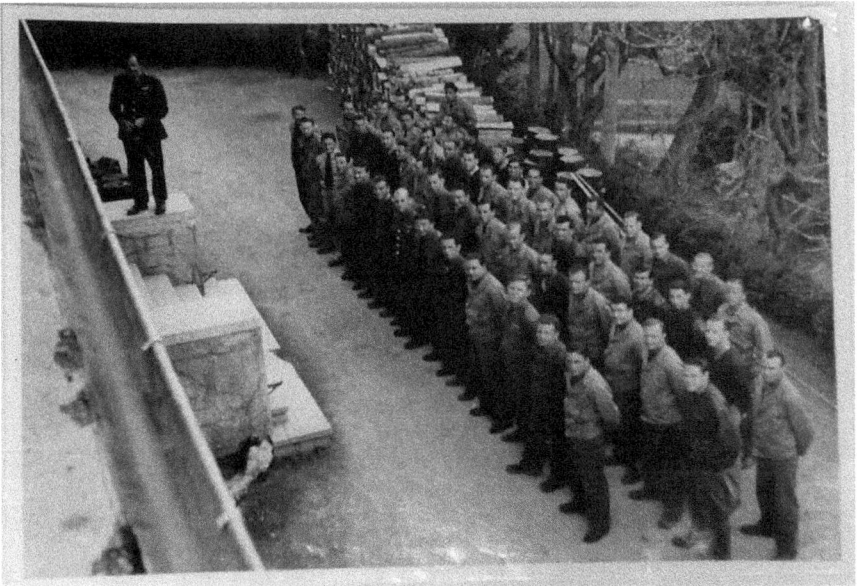

Figure 71. Picture of interned soldiers in Switzerland.
Ken is the second from the right in the back row.

c/o Agence Central Des

Prisonniers de Guerre

Geneva, Switzerland

March 23, 1944:

Dear Mom and Pop:

153

Well here I am in Switzerland right in the middle of the prettiest scenery in the world, the middle of the Alps. The name of the place we are at is Adelboden. I don't know whether or not this will get mailed out today but I thought I would at least start a letter to you.

You are probably wondering why I am here and in what way I arrived. The morning after I wrote my last letter I was up early for another mission. We left early and at the target got pretty well shot up. The plane was full of holes. We were unable to return to our base as gas was leaking all over the place, and we would have bailed out except for Miltner our Waist Gunner who was shot all to pieces. He is in the hospital and we don't know whether or not he will live. One of the officers told us about an hour ago that he was holding his own but if he did live he would probably be a cripple for the rest of his life as his spine is cut in two. It may be better if he didn't live. He had a big hole in his neck, his arm was almost torn off and leg and stomach were all cut up. He sure was a mess. The other Waist Gunner, Childs, had a hole in his arm but he is all right and at present is carrying his arm around in a sling. All the rest of us are all right. It is only through the grace of God we are alive today. We can't understand yet why we didn't explode in midair.

Figure 72. A brochure for the hotel Ken stayed at in Adelboden.

We are interned for the duration of the war over here. You don't have to worry about me as we are being treated all right. We are living in a hotel surrounded by the mountains. There is snow everywhere now although the snow season is nearing the end. The food is good, the meat being rationed. We have dark bread and cocoa almost every morning, along with cheese. For dinner plenty of potatoes usually fried, vegetables and some meat. Supper is light, noodles, macaroni, etc. We can get things at the PX like candy, except chocolate candy which is rationed and fruit, oranges and bananas.

We can get pass privileges now and then and travel to some of the cities over here. We are allowed to wear civilian clothes if we want to. I am going to try and pick up a few souvenirs for you all if I can. At present we are restricted to the hotel for three weeks due to quarantine measures. We don't do much in the hotel but sit around all day. There isn't much to read. I watch the fellows play cards quite often. It is a very monotonous life.

I am only allowed to write two letters a month to my next of kin which will be you, under the present ruling. I can receive letters from anybody. Tell Katy about it so that she can write regularly as I am anxious to hear from her. I will include a line to her in your letters and then you can forward the whole letter to her after showing the letter to the rest of the folks.

There is plenty of skiing going on up here and you can get a swell tan. I will, no doubt, from time to time cable money home to you. Put it in the Five Cents Savings Bank. Also the first of next year, if I am still over here, the Co-Operative Bank is due for another payment and you can pay them another year in advance. I can cable once a week so every once in a while will send you a cable. When you receive any money from me let me know. I am going to enclose a list of addresses and I want you to write them a letter explaining to them that I am interned and cannot write but would like to hear from them every now and then.

We have been going out on a short hike around the mountains here every day. I am planning on going to school here and learning French and German as most of the people speak those two languages.

I don't know what will become of most of my personal stuff back in camp but it is supposed to be kept for me. I will, no doubt, lose a lot of stuff that I really wanted. The only news we get of the outside world here is through the radio, which at present is on the blink.

This typewriter is different from ours in that the z is where the y should be and vice versa, that is why I am always typing z for y. If you have sent any packages to my camp that contained other than candy they will be returned, otherwise I told the fellows to eat the candy up if I didn't come back. In your letters mention nothing about where I came from, and keep the news more or less non-military.

I am going to try and buy a movie camera here as they are much cheaper than those you can get at home and much better.

Tell all the folks not to worry about me. It is too bad I can't write Grandma H. and Katy but that is the rule over here.

I am going to try and get in some skiing up here when our restriction is lifted if I don't break my neck. We will probably be able to go swimming when summer approaches. It is surprising how hot it gets up here with all the snow around.

Coming up to camp here from where we landed we rode on the train. They certainly have some fine trains over here and the coaches are the best. The people here are a very clean people and the cities are the cleanest looking I have ever seen.

Will close for now and finish up later.

Here it is March 30th and I will finish this up as tomorrow we can mail our first letter out.

Figure 73. The American camp in Adelboden was called Camp Moloney, named after Sgt. Joe Moloney, the first American to die on Swiss soil during the war.

Yesterday we had an unpleasant task before us. We were up at 5:30 a.m. and went to Bern to be pall bearers at Miltner's funeral. He died Sunday night at 7:00 p.m. It was a very sad occasion for us as he had been with us a long time and seemed just like a brother. We, the crew, acted as pall bearers. We had a regular military funeral. There were seven large wreaths and they fired the regular 21 gun salute then played Taps. We arrived back here at 8:00 p.m. I was thinking during the funeral service that it could just as well been me or anyone of the crew instead of him but for the Lord's protection. I can't understand how the other Waist Gunner wasn't killed too.

Write as often as you can giving me all the news. Let me know how the Young Peoples Contest is coming along, also how New Bedford High made out in the M.I.T. tournament and how the baseball season progresses, also any other important items of interest. Two weeks from today Wesley will be getting married. Tell me about the wedding, also how his Army status is. It sure seems funny not to be writing every night to you all and receiving letters all the time. I miss the letters more than anything else. Will sure be looking forward to hearing from you. By now you have received my cablegram and am sort of looking for an answer in the next week or two.

Everything we buy here whether in the PX or in the stores is done on credit. We are only allowed a small amount a month to spend in cash, equivalent to around nine dollars a month. Anything else we want we charge it and it is taken out of our account at headquarters here. Every night I have a couple of bottles of orange juice. The other fellows buy beer and liquor.

This just about brings me to the end of the news around here. I will be writing on the fifteenth again and will be out of restriction by then and will no doubt, have more news to write about, although there isn't really much doing around here to write about.

Show these couple of pages to the gang and I am enclosing a sheet of the addresses I want you to write to with a few comments on different ones. Marjorie can write to some of them if she wants to, or you can write to them all.

In the previous letter, Ken asked about Wes' Army status, which might seem strange since Wes ended up in the Navy, but that determination might not have been made until after his induction, just like Ken's placement into the Air Corps was not until after his induction.

Ken mentioned in the previous letter that Miltner did die from his injures. It was an especially bitter moment because the rest of the crew was now safe from combat injures but one of their own had paid the ultimate price. The Swiss government was very understanding in enabling the crew to attend Miltner's funeral and say a final goodbye to a dear comrade.

March 29, 1944:

This was a sad day for us. We had been informed the night before that Miltner had died at 7:00 P.M. Sunday night. He was not in much pain and up until the last few minutes thought he was getting well, as he could move his fingers some, whereas before he was totally paralyzed. We got up at 5:30 A.M. and took the 7:00 A.M. bus to Frutigen where we caught the 8:00 A.M. train to Bern. We had a Swiss M.P. with us for a guard. We were at the American Legation for a couple of hours and then went down to the Hotel Baren with Captain Free and some of the other Officers working in Bern. We were driven around in a German car. The name of it was Opal. We then left for Munsingen where Miltner was to be buried. We had a regular military funeral with 21-gun salutes by the Swiss Soldiers. There were seven large wreaths from various legations at the grave. It was very sad that we had to lose one of our crew on this our last mission in the E.T.O. (European Theater of Operations). We arrived back at the hotel at 8:00 P.M. realizing the heartbreaks that this terrible war has caused. Miltner was married and had two fine children, a boy and a girl around four and five years of age.

Figure 74. 21 gun salute at Miltner's funeral.

With April approaching, the winter season was winding down. Ken was able to take in watching some ski jumping and even tried skiing himself with very mixed results.

March 30, 1944:

In the afternoon we went over to the ski jump to see the championship of Adelboden. I saw the champion of Switzerland, who lives in Adelboden, jump 57 meters or 185 feet. Six other kids participated and one jumped 50 meters. Most of the kids were from twelve to sixteen years of age.

April 5, 1944:

Were informed in the morning that we could go skiing in the afternoon if we wanted to with a guide. Laing and I went down to Perrin's and had a pair of skis fixed up for us. We rented them for a week being rather optimistic. We had a lot of fun and I did pretty good considering everything. Of course, I managed to get three skinned fingers out of the afternoon recreation. It sure was a lot of fun.

April 6, 1944:

I went skiing in the morning again. I sprained my ankle in the morning and it was hurting quite a bit, however, like all Americans are crazy if you ask me, I decided to go again in the afternoon. I wasn't satisfied with just skiing around down below but decided to go way up on top of the mountain by the ski lift. I fell half way up, but managed to get back on again. On reaching the top I started down. It normally takes ten to fifteen minutes. It took me actually two hours. I don't know how many times I fell down and on one of the spills I really did myself up properly. I thought I had broken my ankle. It was just a sprain though and it started swelling up quite a bit. I finished skiing down the mountain and turned my skis in, deciding I had had enough skiing. Skiing was almost over with anyway and so I thought I had better quit before I broke my neck. It sure was a lot of fun though and I wish the season had just been starting rather than closing.

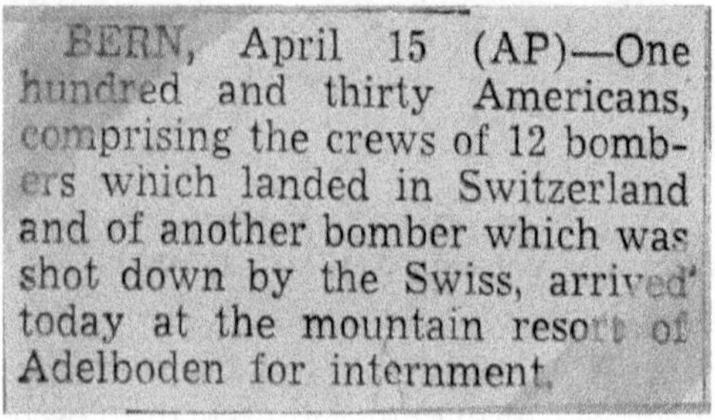

> BERN, April 15 (AP)—One hundred and thirty Americans, comprising the crews of 12 bombers which landed in Switzerland and of another bomber which was shot down by the Swiss, arrived' today at the mountain resort of Adelboden for internment.

Figure 75. An article on some additional American crews going to Adelboden for internment.

Ken and a fellow internee were able to do some exploring and the scenery was probably spectacular.

April 16, 1944:

In the afternoon Ham and I walked up to the top of the mountain in the back of our hotel and looked down into the valley about ten miles from Adelboden. It sure was a pretty sight. It took us about an hour and a half to walk up and about an hour to come down. The top was still covered with snow and of course we managed to get ourselves pretty wet around the feet.

April 23, 1944:

In the afternoon Earl Kendall, Ham and myself took a walk over to the cable car and went up to the top of another mountain. At times we were suspended in mid-air by just a wire a thousand feet above the ground. The car holds four, two on one side and two facing the other two. It takes about six minutes I believe, and most of the time there is quite a drop below you. I took a few pictures and hope they came out good. It is very pretty up on top of the mountain which has snow just about twelve months of the year. You can see miles ahead down the valley.

April 24, 1944:

In the morning I went to my French class. It was my first time and I believe I will like it. Have heard some rumors lately that I may get a chance to go to Bern and work for the American Legation. Sure hope so as it will mean being in a city instead of here in a small place, although it is real nice up here.

Ken's brother Wes married Ellora on April 15, 1944, while Ken was interned. Wes had also been drafted and shortly after the wedding he was in the Navy. A brother's wedding is a significant milestone, and missing it because of the war is just another example of the many sacrifices that were made by so many of the soldiers who fought for our country.

During his extended time training and the various locations at which he had been stationed, Ken had developed a large network of friends. He had been stationed in Illinois, Utah, Florida, Idaho, and Iowa, and connected with individuals in all of these locations, as well as corresponding with letters. With his plane shot down, and the limitations on writing letters, people all across the country had letters returned indicating that Ken was Missing in Action.

May 7, 1944, Letter from Dud:

The letters sent to England by people all over the country must be coming back. The people in Sioux City think you are missing because their letters are coming back marked missing. Rev. Miller of the church there sent Ma a beautiful letter about you. He said some of the finest things anybody could say about a person. Also received a long letter from Esther in which she said you were a wonderful Christian and anybody seeing you would have no doubt about it. She said you helped her go deeper in her Christian experience. … I felt so happy when I read those letters that I had a hard time keeping the tears back. KEEP PRAYING AND READ YOUR BIBLE IF YOU HAVE ONE. We at home will continue to pray for you. I'll bet when you come home you will want to take a trip around the country and visit all of God's people who have been so good to you. I'll bet you have more people praying for you than any other man in the armed forces. I guess we will both have to pray that the war will soon end. … Keep true to Jesus and we will meet by and by. … P.S. Keep praying for me as I need it now more than ever as it won't be long before I'll be graduating from high school and I will have to make my choice for life. I graduate in February.

To the many friends who have corresponded with Technical Sergeant Milfred Kenneth Hathaway, Jr., of New Bedford, Mass. (former president of the N.Y.P.S.), who has been stationed "somewhere in England," and doing missions on a bomber, we wish to inform you that he is now interned in a neutral country. We know that he will be glad to hear from his many acquaintances whom he met and corresponded with during his twenty-one months in the service of his country. If you desire his address, write to his mother, and she will be glad to send his "Prisoner of War Mail" address. He may receive mail but his writing of letters is "limited." His mother's address: Mrs. Mildred K. Hathaway, 108 Pierce St., New Bedford, Mass.

Figure 76. Short article from the Herald of Holiness letting friends know that Ken was now interned in a neutral country. This appeared in the May 29, 1944 issue of the Nazarene publication.

Ken did get the job working as a typist and payroll secretary for the military attaché, American Legation, in Bern Switzerland. He was one of about 13 internees working for the military attaché's office. Included with the materials preserved from the war were a number of mission reports from other crews, similar to the reports that the senior members of Ken's crew had to write following their March 18, 1944, mission. As a typist for the military attaché, it is assumed that Ken may have been the one to type these reports for the official record. His job also may have played a role in his getting access to the reports on their ill-fated mission from his own crew which were included in the previous chapter.

May 24, 1944:

Well I finally got the job. One reason was my typing speed. There was no one in Adelboden or any of the other camps that could match that. I left on the 10:50 A.M. bus for Bern, along with Hildebrand. We hung around the Legation building for a while and then went out to lunch. We made reservations at the Hotel Baren for the time being and then proceeded to get out of our G.I. clothes into civilian clothes as we were not allowed to wear G.I. clothes in Bern.

Once Ken got the job at the military attaché, he moved to Bern for the week and traveled back to Adelboden on the weekend. He was working up to 6 days a week from 8:00 A.M. to 6:00 P.M. with a couple hours off in the middle of the day for lunch.

Figure 77. Swiss cemetery for foreign soldiers.

Memorial Day is a day to honor those who lost their lives in various conflicts while serving their country, so it is not surprising that in the middle of a war, surviving crew members would gather together to honor their friends who paid the price with their lives.

May 30, 1944:

We left at 9:30 A.M. for Munsingen where we held our Memorial Day Service for the 32 fliers buried there. It was very impressive and the pictures in the photograph sections along with description of the ceremony shows what it was like. It was rather sad, especially when you think that these 32 represent only a very small percentage of those buried all over the world in foreign countries.

Even some of those which Ken met stateside shared their Memorial Day stories.

May 30, 1944, letter from Esther in Sioux City:

Last week we added another gold star to our honor roll. A boy was killed in a crash here in the states. He was buried yesterday. Sad part of the whole situation was that the boy didn't know God as his own personal Savior unless he did before he actually went down. Slim chance on that, though. It pays to keep right and to keep prayed up.

Last Sunday evening we dedicated our N.Y.P.S. service to the boys in service. It was a beautiful service. We made mention of the boys that have actually sacrificed on our honor roll. Of course all of them have. Your name was mentioned. Much as you may try not to be one of us – well you've left your influence behind and everyone thinks a lot of you (including me). Eleane's the one that mentioned you. So there – ha! Guess I don't do all the talking about you.

I'm still remembering you in prayer. Keep on believing and soon this will all be over.

An interesting aspect of being interned in Switzerland was that censors from both sides looked over the mail. There were letters returned because of references to military personal or other military information. Mimeographed information was not allowed. Also, anything that promoted one side of the war was prohibited. The letter in Figure 78 was returned because the stamps used were Victory stamps, and forbidden for prisoner of war (POW) mail.

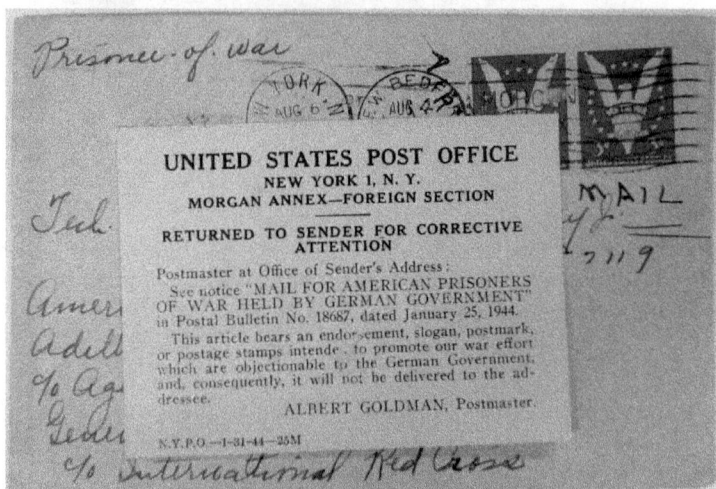

Figure 78. Mail returned because of censor.

D-Day finally arrived, and even though Ken and the others were in Switzerland, they were aware that the invasion had started.

June 6, 1944:

INVASION – that long awaited day has arrived. I sure hope that it means the end of this terrible war very soon. We have been here almost three months and it hardly seems that long, although when we think of when we were home last it seems like years.

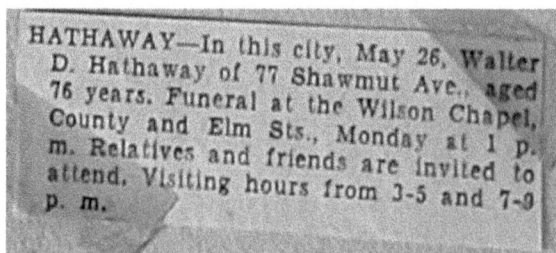

Figure 79 Announcement of Ken's grandfather's funeral.

Another family moment that Ken missed while overseas was the passing of his paternal grandfather. The passages below are portions of a letter Ken's grandmother sent him shortly after her husband's passing.

June 15, 1944, letter from Ken's grandmother:

It is a long time since I heard from you. But when your mother hears from you she brings it up for me to read. God bless her. I cannot seem to realize Grandpa has passed on. This home is very lonely without him.

I do hope God will spare me to see your smiling face once more at home. So watch your step Kenneth. With love from Grandma H.

Figure 80. Swiss cemetery for foreign soldiers.

Ken must have fallen into a routine and forgotten to update the journal or diary he was keeping while in Switzerland. But another unhappy day had arrived with the loss of more flyers. An even more bitter day was on the horizon.

July 17, 1944:

I have slipped up in keeping this up. This is a sad day as we went to Munsingen in the afternoon to bury three more American fliers. To think I too may have been buried there if it was not for the Grace of God. He sure has been good to me and I will never cease to praise Him for it. We also heard that four more planes had landed and that two more are dead. They will undoubtedly be buried within the next couple of days. One of the fellows his parachute failed to open. It certainly must have been a horrible death.

July 20, 1944:

Received this afternoon more sad news. Lt. Smith, our Navigator, had died at Davos in the hospital. Have felt very depressed ever since and could not even eat supper. I thought a lot of him as did all of our crew. He was one of the finest fellows in the crew. He died of an operation, which I believe was intestinal trouble. We also heard five more planes landed and so far have received reports that one is dead.

Figure 81. The New Testament and Psalms Ken kept with him during the war. It had been given to him on 8/4/1942 by Mr. & Mrs. Ainsworth.

The loss of a crew member who was not even injured during their ill-fated raid must have been a bitter pill to swallow. Blood poisoning was eventually given as the leading factor in Smith's death.

Ken always carried his New Testament (King James Version) with him, including on all missions, which meant he still had access to God's Word while he was interned after being shot down.

July 17, 1944, letter home to family:

I have my New Testament with me as I always carried it on every mission I went.

With Ken being relatively safe now in Switzerland, the family's concern turned to Wes who had been drafted and was training in the Navy, but since this letter was to Ken, no specific information could be given as to his location. Wes and his recent bride Ellora were also expecting their first child.

Also the mention of Marge going out with Erland is of note because they eventually married.

July 27, 1944, letter from Mother:

We received two cards from Wes yesterday and two more today. On yesterday's cards he said that he was in a drug store and it was 6 0'clock. He was due back to there at 8 giving him two hrs. off. He said that on July 25th it was a tough day. He got very warm and tired. He reached his destination about noon yesterday – the same place Dwight went to.

Ellora has not told her that she is in the family way. Her mother keeps questioning her about her pains in her side etc.

Marj went out with Erland.

Surprisingly, there were no letters or significant mentions of Katy while Ken was in Switzerland.

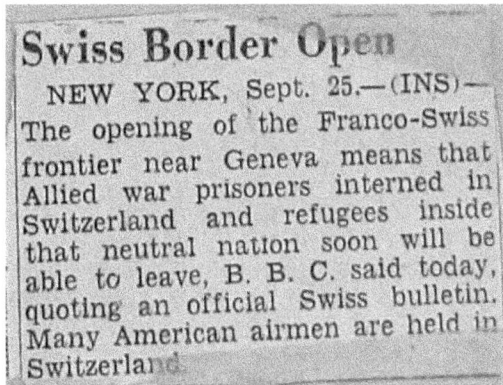

Swiss Border Open

NEW YORK, Sept. 25.—(INS)— The opening of the Franco-Swiss frontier near Geneva means that Allied war prisoners interned in Switzerland and refugees inside that neutral nation soon will be able to leave, B. B. C. said today, quoting an official Swiss bulletin. Many American airmen are held in Switzerland.

Figure 82. Swiss border open.

Prisoner of war camps were not pleasant and were often horrific, but being interned in a neutral country was not nearly as bad; in some cases, the accommodations were charming, even luxurious. The American flyers were put up in a resort hotel which had recently been built. With the war encompassing most of Europe, the Swiss were about the only clientele for the hotel so it was converted to house foreign soldiers. A newspaper article back in the States on the topic of Swiss internees even had the title, "War is no Hell To U.S. Flyers Swiss Interned. American Aviators Live at Resort, Have 'College' and Sports Facilities." It was certainly true that the confines were not as demanding as those of prisoners of war in German camps, but the Swiss internees still had the loss of complete freedom. A gilded cage is still a cage.

A letter dated February 10, 1945, with a subject line of Evacuation of Internees, is the only information preserved that related to the internees leaving Switzerland and returning home, but the actual return appears to have started significantly later. The exact date Ken was able to start home is not known.

Switzerland Interns 1,500 U. S. Airmen

WASHINGTON, Dec. 23 (AP) —Some 1,500 U. S. airmen forced down during bombing missions to Germany had been interned in Switzerland up to Oct. 1, the Swiss legation said today.

A total of about 95,000 refugees of 20 nationalities had been admitted to switzerland on that date.

The American airmen were among 16,000 military internees. Other refugee classes are: 48,500 civilians from adjacent war zones; 18,500 former Italian soldiers; 7,500 emigrants blocked by the war from proceeding to their destination; 3,300 escaped prisoners of war; 700 deserters from various armies and 500 soldiers of various countries, hospitalized in Switzerland by their governments.

Figure 83. Article on the Swiss internees.

Ken received a commendation from the military attaché in Switzerland for his service during his time as an internee.

THE MILITARY ATTACHÉ
Legation of the
United States of America
Bern, Switzerland
16 February 1945

SUBJECT: Commendation

TO: T/Sgt. Milfred K. Hathaway, 31157119, U.S.A.A.F.

I wish to make of record the service which you have voluntarily rendered during the period of your internment in Switzerland, which should distinguish you and be of value to your military record and reputation.

From May 24, 1944 to date, you rendered valuable service to my office in finance work for which you were equipped by your previous experience in civil life.

I have personal knowledge of your loyalty and willingness to serve. Regardless of the tasks assigned you, this work has been performed efficiently and accurately, frequently under great stress.

In addition to this official recognition, I wish to add my personal appreciation of your helpful cooperation and extend to you my very best wishes for a continued successful career.

B. R. Legge
Brigadier General, U.S.A.
Military Attaché

The war was slowly coming to an end. VE Day —the day of victory in Europe—was May 8, 1945, and it is likely that around that time Ken was either on his way home or about to leave shortly for the trip back to the States.

Chapter 11

Back Home/Engagement

The war in Europe was over. Hitler's forces had been defeated by the combined might of the Allied forces. It was time for the soldiers to start to make their way back to their home countries. There is no information on the exact date when Ken was able to leave Switzerland and start the trip home to the States. Ken's brother Dud shared that Ken traveled on board the RMS Mauretania 2. The original Mauretania was a sister ship to the Lusitania, which was sunk near the beginning of World War I by a German U-boat (May 7, 1915). Dud shared that one of the things Ken did on his return trip was to help feed a soldier who had lost both of his arms during the war, which must have been quite an experience. The trip across the Atlantic probably took several weeks.

Figure 84. The Mauritania 2, picture taken by Ken's brother Dud.

Later in life, while Dud served as a chaplain in the Navy he was on a destroyer which docked in Naples, Italy on May 3, 1963. In traveling from the destroyer to the shore on a motor whale boat (the small boat carried on destroyers for this purpose), Dud looked up at a large boat they were passing by and saw the name Mauretania, the very ship his brother had traveled home on from the war. The picture in Figure 84 is from that day.

Even though the war in Europe was over, and Ken had returned to the States, the war in the Pacific was still going on and Ken was still in the Army Air Corps. He ended up stationed at Scott Field in Illinois, the location he probably requested and was most interested in because of its proximity to St. Louis and Katy.

June 26, 1945:

Well here I am at Scott Field. Tomorrow I start working as typist over in headquarters. I work from 7:30 A.M. until 4:30 P.M. I get a pass every night and have Sundays off.

We left Sat. (from Atlantic City) at 1:30 P.M. and I got into St. Louis at 6:15 P.M. Sunday night. Katy met me at the station. She waited over an hour for me as we were late.

Ken's brother Wes had been drafted into the Navy, but the war in Europe had wrapped up and the war in the Pacific was winding down. Wes was fortunate in that he never did have to participate in combat.

July 3, 1945:

I understand Wes may be heading for the South Pacific soon. I sure hope not but if so know that the Lord will protect him over there and bring him back safely to us all. We have a great God and He can handle every situation.

July 12, 1945:

I heard Wes may get home before he goes across. If he does I am going to try and get home too, as I want to see him. I sure hope he can get home for a few days.

Being stationed at Scott Field, Ken got to see Katy regularly and he asked her to marry him. She accepted, though the date of the engagement is not clear from the materials that were saved. But this turned out to be a challenging time for their relationship for several reasons. One of the challenges was that Katy was unwilling to set a date for the wedding.

July 3, 1945:

Have nothing definite to report on the marriage date but hope it is in September so you can all come out. Ought to know very soon on that.

July 6, 1945:

I don't know when I am going to get married yet and probably will not know for another month. However, I will know in time to let you know and as soon as I know definitely will let you know so you can bring the car out in September if I am getting married and if not you can bring the car out in August. Will probably know by the end of the month anyway.

July 16, 1945:

Will know about my getting married September 8th the end of the month for sure. Hope I do as then you can all come out.

Another challenge was that the values of some in the area (and some of the family) were very conservative, even for Christians in the Midwest in the 1940s. Even Katy's mom had strong views about a couple holding hands when they were not yet married.

July 19, 1945:

Wednesday night, or last night we had the annual election of Officers, at church. ... The minister's assistant gave a talk on boys and fellows running around and seemed to be hinting at Katy. Of course that included me. Bro. Rosch doesn't believe that you should even touch a girl you are going with while in church. I mean put your hand on her shoulder or anything like that. He is very narrow. He doesn't believe you should kiss a girl, and it is said he kissed his wife only once before they were married. What a courtship they must have had. Anyway Katy felt quite bad and it looks like things are going to break real soon.

July 27, 1945, letter to Mom:

Thanks for your opinion on the subject, that I asked you about. I got pretty peeved Sunday with Mom (Katy's Mom) because she stopped us from walking up the street holding hands. Katy said she didn't see anything wrong with it but her mother says it isn't nice and she would never hold hands with her husband when they were courting. Her mother sensed that I didn't like it and that Katy also didn't like it because after the evening service while we were in the kitchen she came in and apologized, but said she still thinks we shouldn't hold hands and thought it was settled when she told us so the other night.

July 30, 1945, letter to Aunt Annie:

Katy's mother believes it doesn't look right for us to hold hands walking down the street. We still do it, except when walking to church Sundays and then sometimes we do it then. I don't think they object to me, at least I know Pop doesn't any way. I don't know whether her mother has changed or not in regards to her wanting me to marry Katy but I don't think so, she only wants us to wait for a year or so, but Katy says she isn't going to do that. Katy mentioned settling a date in November. I told her if she wanted November she would have to set the date, but that I wanted September and that would be the only date I would set. If it wasn't for the folks coming out here November would be good because I could get an 18 day furlough then and have a nice honeymoon whereas in September I can't. However, the Lord will work things out for the best and I am letting Him have His way in the matter.

But the biggest issue was that Katy never told her other boyfriend about the engagement. As stated earlier, Katy had been dating another fellow, Delton, who was also away in the service when she met Ken. They had been dating, but they were apparently not exclusively dating each other, which had given the window of opportunity initially for Ken to share his interest in Katy. Though Katy said she loved Ken and wanted to marry him, she was unwilling to break it off with Delton, hence the refusal on setting a wedding date.

It is easy for outsiders to look on this whole situation as foolish, but the intoxicating nature of young love has derailed common sense in many an individual. It is also hard to put ourselves in a situation where not only these challenges exist, but also the emotionally charged context of it happening in the midst of a war where many soldiers would not be returning home. The letters below are just a few that share some of the challenges and struggles because of Katy's unwillingness to break it off clean with Delton.

July 23, 1945:

I wish you would do me a favor Dud and that is pray for Katy and me. Katy says she knows she loves me and that she will be happy married to me but that she doesn't know just when to get married. She wants to get married in September but somehow when she prays about it she can't make the connection. She said the Lord led her to decide in my favor and she believes the Lord can work things out so that she can break with Delton without causing any hard feelings. ... If you get the time I would like you to write Katy a letter of some kind as I know she would appreciate it. It seems lately no one in the family has written to her as they are sort of peeved because she won't decide to marry me in September. I still love her with all my heart and believe everything is in the Lord's hands and he will work things out for the best.

July 27, 1945, letter to Mom:

Katy told me last night she definitely didn't love Delton at all, because I told her if she did, or if I thought she did I would break off right now. She said she is definitely going to marry me and it would break her heart if I would break off. She says she believes the Lord can work everything out and that she is praying daily for the Lord to undertake and tell her what to do. She wants to marry me real bad and feels terrible about the whole situation, but she says she didn't pray about the other love affair of hers and she wasn't going to do anything until the Lord definitely spoke to her and revealed when she should marry me. I have only been in once this week and am giving her time to think it over. She said last night that she asked the Lord to please let her know by Saturday so she could give me an answer. I don't know what will happen, or whether anything definite will come out of it or not. I told her I would leave her if she wants Delton and she says she doesn't want Delton, that she wants only me, so there you are.

July 30, 1945, letter to Aunt Annie:

I went in and saw Katy that night. She didn't receive that letter from Delton Saturday but has settled it, in that the day she receives that letter she will write him and tell him that they are finished and that she is engaged to me. She settled that either Friday or Saturday and when I went in Saturday night was really happy over the situation. She felt good and we had a swell weekend together.

To be clear, Delton knew about Ken; they even had met previously when Ken was stationed at Scott Field during his training; Ken had actually been to the Delton's house at that time. But as the relationship between Ken and Katy turned serious, Katy had never told Delton about the engagement.

July 30, 1945, letter to Aunt Annie:

I don't think Delton's folks have ever said a word to Delton about the matter nor he to them. Delton knows all about the situation except Katy being engaged to me. He knows she went home with me, that I spent my furloughs with her, that I am stationed out here permanently and that she goes out with me every night, but he has never told his folks because they have hinted that he doesn't know anything about it. They are very closed mouthed the family and not very close and they don't confide in one another. The only reason Delton doesn't say anything is that he knows if he does that it will cause him to lose Katy so he is keeping quiet hoping it will blow over.

Most of the folks in the church are for me, at least that is what they say. The Wakefields think she is crazy not to get married no matter what some folks may say, also the Masons and Betty who is Katy's friend thinks Katy is crazy to hold off getting married and there are quite a few others. The Assistant Pastor even asked me when we were going to get married as he wanted to play at our wedding.

August 23, 1945:

I have realized for a long time that my mistake was in becoming engaged to Katy before she broke with Delton but it is something that nothing can be done about now. It looks like I am in a tough position, but as I told Ma I expect Katy to break her engagement to me this Sunday night so then everything will be settled. I still can't see Katy marrying Delton because she admits she would be happier with me and she seems to think more spiritual, and I am sure the Lord would want her to be happier and more spiritual so I can't figure the thing out. I have given up any way and am only waiting for her to make the break which is coming very soon. I thought it was coming last night but it didn't. So it looks like I will be seeing you all very soon.

Write again when you have time and it looks like I will have to come up to E.N.C. and find a wife. Ha.

Ken's brother Wes was in the Navy now training for the war in the Pacific. Wes's wife Ellora kept in touch in Ken and gave him what updates she could, along with sharing about their son, Ken's new nephew, Wesley Jr.

Birthday card from Ellora, 1945:

We are all praying for you and we pray that you will have your dreams come true real soon. I heard for the last time from Wesley yesterday and guess it'll be quite some time before I hear again. Please pray for him and know that God is able to see him thru. Baby is fine and getting bigger and cuter all of the time. He sure has brought a lot of joy and comfort to me and I'm so glad he's here. God has been good to me and us and love him more tonite than I ever had. I never will cease to trust in him.

Wes served his country in the Navy, and thankfully never did see any combat. His boot camp training was in Sampson, NY, and at some point he was in Panama before shipping out to Pearl Harbor. He was a third-class gunner's mate and may have served on the YMS-138 which was a minesweeper ship. He was discharged in early 1946.

Dud was really a rock of spiritual advice, fitting for one who would go on to spend his life in ministry.

Birthday card from Dud, 1945:

I am sorry that things are turning out the way they are. I think you should settle things one way or another <u>very soon</u>. Give her a deadline on writing a letter and make sure it gives the story. She seems to hurt your feelings but won't hurt his. Have been praying daily for you and am trusting the Lord for complete victory. Make your surrender complete and if the Lord should call you, you will be happy and willing to do His will. Don't think it was easy for me to answer the call of the Lord, I fought it for at least two years. Then I came to the place where I had to give up all together or do His will. Just a little over a year ago on Aug 6, 1944, I told the Lord I would do whatever He wanted me to do. It meant giving up ambitions, plans etc. and it wasn't easy but today I would feel like I was out of place if I was doing something else. I am happy serving Him and if He should see fit to send me to the uttermost parts of the earth, I am ready to go. When God has called you and you have given all to Him you will be the happiest person in the world and you won't care where He leads you. Be sure God has called you before you do anything but when he does do not hesitate to answer the call.

Keep holding on to God and keep praying. Will continue to pray for you and trust that God will meet your need. Life is short at its longest and what more can we do for the One who died for us on Calvary. I shall be the happiest fellow in the world when I receive the good news of God's answer to our prayers. One who is praying for you always.

P.S. Remember, God will see you through if He calls you.

The war was finally completely over. The Japanese surrendered on August 15, 1945, after the second atomic bomb was dropped, though the declaration of the ending of hostilities was not signed until September 2, 1945, onboard the battleship USS Missouri in Tokyo Bay.

On the romance front, the inevitable happened: Katy broke up with Ken.

September 5, 1945:

As you know by now Katy broke with me Monday night. I still can't figure out the Lord's hand in this. If she had broken off a week earlier I could have been stationed near home as it was I am too late to get a transfer by a week. It looks as though the Lord wants me here.

While Ken and Katy did get back together for a while after the break-up, the challenges of this relationship proved too much. Ken eventually realized that it was better for him to just move on.

Discharged

Discharged at Randolph Field, Texas:
KENWORTHY, William, staff sergeant, 27 Keene Street, New Bedford.

Discharged at Marine Headquarters, Washington:

FINLEY, William E., sergeant, 45 Green Street, Fairhaven.

Discharged at Sampson, N. Y.:
JONES, Warren H., yeoman 1st class, 348 Coffin Avenue, New Bedford.

Discharged at Westover Field:
SULLIVAN, Daniel F., 1st lieutenant, 674 Cottage Street, New Bedford.

Discharged from A.A.F. at Fresno, Cal.:
ASHLEY, Maynard W., sergeant, Box 204A, R.F.D. 2, New Bedford.

Discharged from A.A.F. at Scott Field, Ill.:

HATHAWAY, Milfred K. Jr., technical sergeant, 108 Pierce Street, New Bedford.

Discharged at Fort Devens:
LEBLANC, George A., technical sergeant, 64 Waldo Street, New Bedford.

Discharged from A.A.F. at Truax Field, Wis.:

McKAY, Arthur S., staff sergeant, 212 Harwich Street, New Bedford.

Discharged from A.A.F. at Stuttgart, Ark.:

SAMSON, Joseph A., sergeant, 14 Crompton Street, Acushnet.

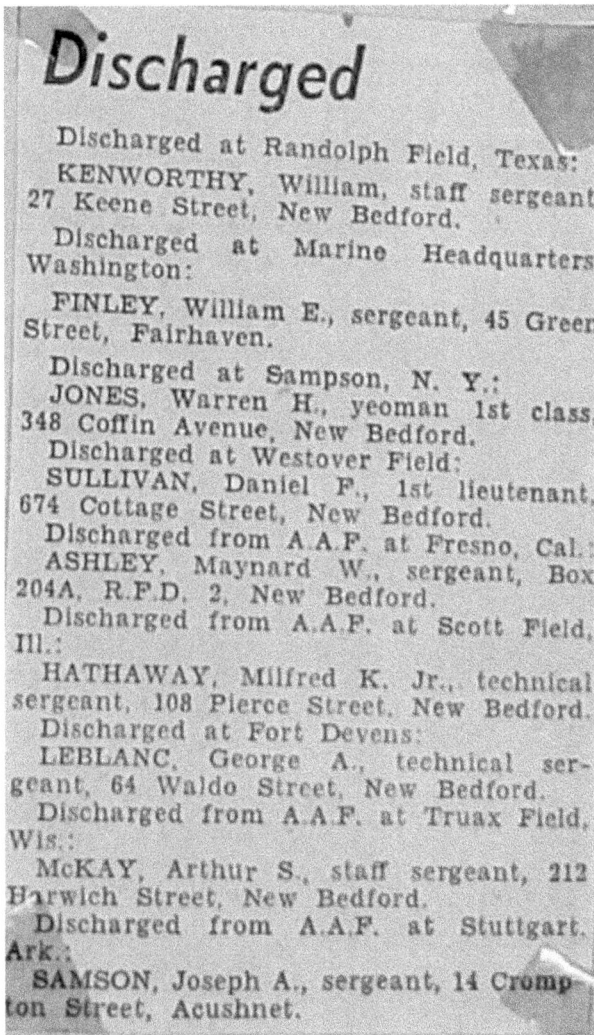

Figure 85. Article showing discharged soldiers.

Ken was honorably discharged on October 26, 1945. He spent a bit of time traveling and visiting many he had met and with whom he developed relationships through his time in the service.

Ken's brother Dud shared that one person Ken visited in early 1946 was the man who had lost both arms in an explosion, whom Ken had befriended and had fed on the ocean trip back to the States.

One last official piece of mail from the Army referenced confidentiality restrictions being lifted.

Letter from Army Air Forces Headquarters, postmarked February 23, 1946:

If you have been sworn to secrecy as a result of your escape, evasion or internment, you may consider yourself released from all restrictions as to disclosure or publication or experiences except:

    a) Secret intelligence activities and methods developed for use, or actually used, in prison camps.

    b) Details of techniques employed by military intelligence organizations operating behind enemy lines to assist evasion and escape.

    c) Negotiations conducted on high government or military level to secure release for internment in a neutral country (See AAF Reg 46-8 dated 30 October 1945).

Chapter 12

Post-War Life

Ken and Katy may have broken up, but he always remained close to the Babb family. My parents took several trips across the country and rarely stayed in motels because they had so many friends scattered across the country with whom they stayed. I can still remember a cross-country trip when I was still living at home, probably early high school age. On this trip we stopped in St. Louis and stayed with the Babb family. So I got to meet "Mom and Pop" Babb. Their daughter Katy lived in the area and stopped by during our visit, so I even got to meet Katy (though at the time I did not realize the significance of the connection). I even have in my house today an afghan that Mom Babb made which I was given on that cross-country trip. So many break-ups end in bitterness, so it was encouraging to see that although Ken and Katy did not end up together, the other relationships developed because of romance remained positive and strong.

In case you are curious as to what happened to Katy, she did eventually marry Delton and they remained in the St. Louis area. Delton passed away in 1982 and Katy passed away in 2004.

My father left a wonderful example in his continued relationship with the Babb family. Broken romantic relationships are never fun, and rarely pleasant, yet here we have an example showing that when a relationship is fractured and shattered it does not need to end in bitterness and hate.

As a Christian who follows a Lord that loves us all, this is how I would expect the Lord would want us to respond. The hurt may remain, but so does the Christian example.

After returning to New Bedford, Ken joined his youngest brother Dud at Eastern Nazarene College (ENC) in Quincy, MA. After Ken being in the military and away for so long, it was probably a nice opportunity for the two brothers to spend some time together.

Ken was able to go to college on the GI bill and majored in mathematics with plans to become a high school mathematics teacher. While at ENC, he met and married a biology major, Ruth Bass, from the Springfield, MA area. Ken graduated in three years, in 1949, alongside his brother Dud and Dud's wife Faith. Ruth had graduated the previous year. By the time of his graduation from ENC, Ken had already started taking graduate courses at Boston University and in 1950 graduated with a MA in mathematics education.

Ken and Ruth spent a short time in western Massachusetts, having two daughters, Cheryl and Joy. Ken eventually took a job as a mathematics teacher at Stratford High School in Stratford, CT, moving the family down to the coast of Connecticut and settling in Milford, CT. Their son, Dale Kenneth, was born in Milford to complete the family.

Ken was a very successful high school mathematics teacher. He rose to become the department head, and a few years later, when another high school was added to the town, he was asked to also oversee the mathematics department at that high school. In addition to his full time job as mathematics department chair at two high schools, he also taught for years as an adjunct at Housatonic Community College, working for a faculty member who had been one of his high school students. So at the peak of his career he not only was simultaneously the head of the mathematics departments at two high schools, but also was a regular adjunct at the local community college.

Ken always wanted to return to Switzerland, and eventually he did. After retirement, Ken and Ruth made numerous trips overseas, and on one occasion went on a European trip that included a short stop in Switzerland. The trip was a prepackaged tour and Adelboden was not included, so he was not able to make it all the way back to the location of his internment, but he did get to share the experience of Switzerland with Ruth.

Milfred K. Hathaway Jr.

BRANFORD, Conn. — Milfred Kenneth Hathaway Jr., 82, of Robert Treat Parkway, Milford, died Wednesday, June 13, 2001, at Connecticut Hospice in Branford. He was the husband of Ruth Bass Hathaway.

Born in New Bedford, Mass., the son of the late Milfred K. Hathaway Sr. and Isabel Edith Cunningham Hathaway, he was a resident of Milford for more than 46 years.

Previously, he was a resident of Wollaston, Cheshire and Adams, all in Massachusetts.

Mr. Hathaway was an Army veteran of World War II, where he was a radioman and a bombardier.

He was a recipient of the Bronze Star and was an internee in Switzerland for a year when his airplane was shot down over Germany.

He earned his bachelor of science degree from Eastern Nazarene College, his master's degree from Boston University, and his sixth year degree in mathematics.

Prior to retiring, Mr. Hathaway worked for the Stratford Public School System, where he taught mathematics and was head of the mathematics department for 25 years at Stratford and Bunnell High Schools.

He was also a mathematics teacher at the Housatonic Community College for 25 years and the Christian Heritage School in Trumball for five years.

He was a treasurer of the Nazarene Churches for 51 years and served on the Church Board for 50 years.

He was a member of the Housatonic Teachers Federal Credit Union since 1956. He served on the Board of Directors and was chairman of its supervisory committee.

He was an 11-year member of the Greater Bridgeport Retired Teachers Association.

Mr. Hathaway was a direct descendant of eight passengers who came over on the original voyage of the Mayflower.

Survivors include his widow; two daughters, Cher Hathaway of New Philadelphia, Ohio, and Joy Hathaway and her husband, Richard Fillon, of Hingham, Mass.; a son, Dr. Dale Hathaway, and his wife, Heather, of Bourbonnais, Ill.; two brothers, Chaplain Dudley C. Hathaway of Lexington, Ky., and Wesley Hathaway of Chandler, Ariz.; six grandchildren, Denise Dink of Canton, Ohio, Tessa Shaw of Uhrichsville, Ohio, Charla Shinaberry of Dennison, Ohio, and Lauren, Lindsay and David Hathaway, all of Bourbonnais, Ill.; two great-grandchildren, Olivia Shaw and Josey Diuk; and many nieces and nephews.

He was the brother of the late Marjorie MacKay.

A funeral service will be at 10 a.m. Saturday in the Cody-White Funeral Home, 107 Broad Street on the Green, Milford.

Interment will be at the Baptist Village Cemetery, East Longmeadow, Mass.

Figure 86. One of Ken's obituaries. This obituary says that he received the Bronze Star but there is no evidence of that award and it is unlikely given that it was awarded for ground combat. It probably should have stated the flying medal which he did receive.

Ken's dedication to his Lord never wavered. While the Nazarene churches he attended were fairly small, he played a significant role as a layman, serving as a treasurer for the church for 51 years and as a board member for 50 years.

The one year in which he was not elected to the board stood out as a sore spot for Ken because of some of the politics of the local church. Those issues eventually caused him and Ruth to eventually leave that local Nazarene church, but his connection to the denomination and his faithfulness to the Lord remained strong.

Epilogue

This story has been an attempt to preserve one man's personal account and experiences during World War II. So many of that "Greatest Generation" have left us, but their stories—of courage, fear, and emotion—are our stories. Ken obeyed, served, and proved faithful in fulfilling the duties he was charged to complete.

At one point, I thought of titling this book, *The Liberator*, which would have carried the double referencing of the type of bomber that my father flew on, but also a second deeper meaning. Throughout this book, my dad's commitment to serve his Lord and Savior is evident and weaves throughout the whole narrative, from training days, to challenging missions, to internment in a neutral country. The Liberator is also a name for the One my father followed and served. Knowing the Lord through his son Jesus Christ truly is a liberating experience.

About
Kharis Publishing:

Kharis Publishing, an imprint of Kharis Media LLC, is a leading Christian and inspirational book publisher based in Aurora, Chicago metropolitan area, Illinois. Kharis' dual mission is to give voice to under-represented writers (including women and first-time authors) and equip orphans in developing countries with literacy tools. That is why, for each book sold, the publisher channels some of the proceeds into providing books and computers for orphanages in developing countries so that these kids may learn to read, dream, and grow. For a limited time, Kharis Publishing is accepting unsolicited queries for nonfiction (Christian, self-help, memoirs, business, health and wellness) from qualified leaders, professionals, pastors, and ministers. Learn more at: https://kharispublishing.com/

www.ingramcontent.com/pod-product-compliance
Lightning Source LLC
Chambersburg PA
CBHW051423090426
42737CB00014B/2810